Guid to coffee culture for Hospitality and Enthusiasts

1, Volume 1

Damjan Kralj

Published by Damjan Kralj, 2024.

GUID TO COFFEE CULTURE FOR HOSPITALITY AND ENTHUSIASTS

First edition. July 5, 2024.

Copyright © 2024 Damjan Kralj.

ISBN: 979-8227616555

Written by Damjan Kralj.

Also by Damjan Kralj

1

Guid to coffee culture for Hospitality and Enthusiasts

Standalone

Mastering the Art of Restaurateur: Introducing Skills for Success

Table of Contents

Dedicated to the Hospitality industrie.

GUIDE TO COFFEE CULTURE FOR HOSPITALITY AND ENTHUSIASTS

INTRODUCTION

Coffee is one of the most popular beverages in the world. Everywhere you look, you can see people sitting in cafes enjoying their coffee or rushing to work with a takeaway cup in hand. It's the ultimate morning pleasure.

In my career, I had a wonderful experience working in a global franchise of coffee shops, perhaps one of the most famous in the world. It's not the kind of cafe that offers coffee at the push of a button. It requires the effort of a barista and a team.

I had the honor of managing a coffee shop that ranked second in the world in terms of sales and transactions within that franchise, second only to a cafe in Dubai that held the top spot.

I was also privileged to manage two coffee shops at that time and carry the title of coffee maestro, proudly wearing silver coffee bean pins that distinguished me as such.

As a lover of great quality coffee, along with the successes I achieved in the franchise, coffee has remained a significant passion in hospitality for me. I want to share my knowledge with others and hope it benefits them.

I enjoy teaching young colleagues and watching them become passionate about becoming baristas and engaging in the art of coffee with zeal.

Just like all aspects of the hospitality industry, coffee shops and coffee deserve attention, dedication, and written discussions.

Coffee shops, like all food establishments, must be managed according to food safety standards, especially with the variety of coffees made using different milks, toppings, syrups, liqueurs, and more. Additionally, coffee shops don't just offer the aforementioned items but also sandwiches, croissants, cakes, etc.

COFFEE

Coffee is a beverage made from roasted and ground seeds of evergreen plants of African origin.

It is one of the three most popular drinks in the world.

Coffee is the basis for a wide variety of drinks. Its popularity is mainly attributed to its invigorating effect, produced by caffeine, an alkaloid present in coffee.

It represents one of the most profitable grocery items and one of the most sensitive when contacting other groceries. Proper and safe transportation and storage are necessary to prevent any impact on its quality. It easily absorbs unnecessary and unwanted odors, flavors, and moisture.

Coffee is one of the most sensitive food items in every sense, from transportation, storage, use, and general standards.

It is known as a diuretic.

Two types of coffee plants, Coffea arabica, and C. canephora, supply nearly all global consumption.

Arabica is considered milder, tastier, and more aromatic than Robusta, the main variety of C. canephora.

The flatter and elongated grain of Arabica is more widespread than Robusta, but it is more delicate and susceptible to pests, requiring a lot of moisture and having quite specific requirements, needing to grow at higher altitudes. Latin America, East Africa, Asia, and Arabia are the leading producers of Arabica coffee.

Round Robusta beans are more resistant. It can grow at lower altitudes. Robusta coffee is cheaper to produce, also having double the caffeine content of Arabica, and is usually the grain chosen for inexpensive commercial coffee brands. Western and Central Africa, Southeast Asia, and Brazil are the main producers of Robusta coffee.

Coffee plants likely originated in Kefa, Ethiopia, were transferred to southern Arabia, and cultivated in the 15th century.

How was coffee discovered? According to one legend, an Arab goatherd was puzzled by the strange antics of the herd he was tending and the energy exhibited by the goats. Later, in the 9th century A.D., a goatherd named Kaldi allegedly tried the berries that the goats had been eating, and when he experienced an exhilarating feeling, he shared his discovery further.

Its stimulating effect undoubtedly made it popular.

Coffee was popularized in one country after another during the 16th and 17th centuries. By the end of the 17th century, coffeehouses were thriving across Britain, the British colonies in America, and continental Europe.

By the 20th century, the greatest concentration of production was focused in the Western Hemisphere, particularly in Brazil. By the late 19th and early 20th centuries, industrial machines for roasting and grinding were introduced. Vacuum-sealed containers were invented over time, and methods of decaffeination for green coffee beans were developed. After 1950, the production of instant coffee was perfected, leading to an increase in the production of cheaper Robusta beans in Africa.

Overall, every day, month, and year efforts were made to protect this mentioned world treasure that has already become a people's strong habit worldwide.

ARABICA

When you observe coffee beans, you encounter a great variety.

Different beans have different characteristics that give them their flavor. Perhaps the most famous is Arabica coffee.

Today there are more than 100 different types of coffee. Coffea Arabica and Coffea Canephora (Robusta) are the most well-known. Arabica is more commonly consumed and accounts for 60-70% of the total world production.

Dating back to around 1,000 BC in present-day Ethiopia, the Oromo tribe crushed Arabica coffee beans and mixed them with fat to form small balls that were consumed for increased energy. They had their way of preparing and consuming it.

Arabica got its name when it arrived in lower Arabia around the 7th century, and historical records describe Arab scientists brewing coffee to work longer, ultimately spreading worldwide. This leads us to question how these scientists could work longer, more energetically, and with less sleep.

Arabica coffee beans require higher altitudes, which also contribute to their complex taste and acidity. This could even be compared to the characteristics of wine, where altitude and coffee beans yield results.

The premium characteristics come at a cost for their growers as the increase in altitude also slows down growth, which can impact production and price.

Compared to Robusta coffee, Arabica coffee may take twice as long to grow. Similarly, Arabica coffee trees may take five to seven years to fully mature, while Robusta coffee trees take half the time.

While Arabica coffee thrives at higher altitudes, it can also withstand low temperatures, as expected. Arabica coffee trees will grow fragrant white flowers resembling jasmine for two to four years before producing dark red berries. Sometimes referred to as the "merlot of coffee," Arabica coffee is highly prized for its mild taste often described as light, and airy, with hints of flowers, fruits, or caramel. Its premium taste often makes Arabica coffee beans more expensive than other coffees.

Arabica coffee plantation.[1]

Arabica coffee plantation.[2]

Robusta coffee is characterized as bitter, woody, or leathery due to higher levels of caffeine and chlorogenic acids. Although these qualities may not seem the most desirable, they are known to help Robusta coffee trees be more resistant to pests and insects. Unfortunately, Arabica trees are more susceptible to damage from pests for this reason.

Arabica coffee beans have a better taste because they contain nearly 60 percent more lipids and double the amount of sugar compared to Robusta beans. These qualities not only affect the taste but also the aroma and body of the coffee. The sweetness of the beans not only enhances the taste of the coffee but also provides a better mouthfeel and reduces bitterness, leaving only a subtle aroma.

The foam that forms on top of a cup of coffee is also crucial. The foam is full of aroma, and flavor, and represents the essence of that coffee.

Another significant difference between Arabica and Robusta coffee beans is their appearance. Arabica beans are larger and have an oval shape, while Robusta beans are usually smaller and round.

When it comes to coffee, the most attractive factor is the vast variety of flavors you encounter.

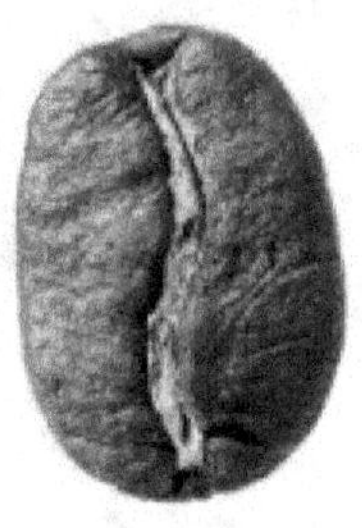

Arabica bean.[3]

ROBUSTA

Robusta coffee, known by its scientific name as coffee canephora, is the second most consumed coffee in the world.

It is one of the two types of coffee consumed worldwide, making up about 40% of the global coffee production.

Robusta coffee grows on bushes and trees with fruits that ripen for processing and drying.

Growing in different climate conditions and altitudes, Robusta coffee is a resilient plant, potentially key to sustainable coffee production in the future due to its natural resistance to pests from its high caffeine content.

Most likely originating from Africa, currently 90% of coffee production in Vietnam is Robusta coffee.

Robusta coffee is known for its intense flavors, containing 60% less sugar and fat than Arabica coffee.

It often presents notes of chocolate and nuts, with a low acidity level.

Special robust coffee contains flavor notes that are rich and complex. Due to its deep flavor profile, robust coffee perfectly complements creamy milk and the sweetness of sugar.

It matures faster than Arabica due to its resilience, which is a blessing for coffee growers. This allows farmers to produce it more quickly to meet the needs worldwide.

Robusta coffee plantations.[4]

Robusta coffee plantations.[5]

It can be found in blends of espresso and instant coffee, as well as in specialty coffee roasts around the world. Robusta coffee is becoming increasingly popular as coffee lovers seek different types of coffee. This allows producers to cultivate and process new varieties of robusta coffee that are unique and flavorful. And what we didn't know is that they can surprise and produce world-class results.

It can be brewed in multiple ways, from drip to espresso. Each brewing style will create a different cup of coffee containing varying levels of oils and unique flavor notes.

Robusta coffee can be consumed with or without milk and sugar. As you drink and enjoy your coffee, you can do the same with robusta coffee.

For those who enjoy a deep, roasted taste when drinking coffee, robusta coffee is highly recommended.

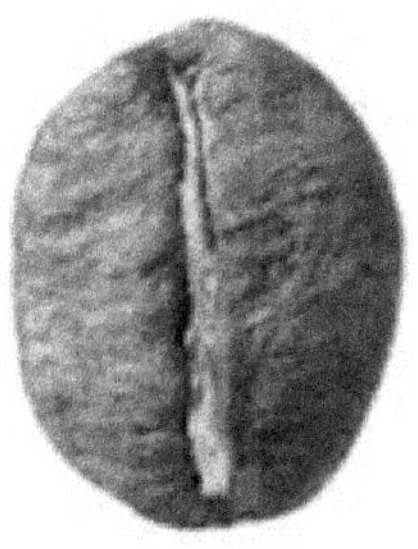

Robusta bean.[6]

LIBERICA COFFEE

Liberica is an unusual and rare coffee in the specialty coffee industry. It is not as popular as Arabica and Robusta coffee. Most new coffee enthusiasts might not even recognize it.

This variety can only be found in certain countries, and it is considered a rare type of coffee that is close to extinction.

Liberica coffee originally comes from the western and central parts of Africa, specifically Liberia, where it first originated in the mid-1800s. It makes up less than 2% of commercially produced coffee worldwide, which explains why it is not as well-known.

This type of coffee is not very popular and is extremely rare in the coffee industry because it is difficult to find and cultivate.

It is an evergreen shrub that grows into a large tree (up to 20 m high), resistant to pests and diseases. It has larger leaves and beans compared to other coffee varieties.

In terms of growth conditions, it is very similar to Robusta, tolerating dry environments and preferring to grow at low altitudes.

Liberica is a type of coffee that has unique characteristics. It is known for its enormous size, density, and weight as a bean. The shape of the bean is irregular, almost almond-shaped.

Liberica coffee plantation.[7]

When it comes to taste, Liberica coffee usually has a better cup quality than Robusta, but is less superior compared to Arabica.

The taste can be described as a unique floral and fruity flavor, with hints of woodiness and earthiness.

Although it has a bitter taste, it contributes to its strong flavor. Filipinos commonly referred to it as "Barako coffee", associating it with masculinity.

Liberica is typically served as black coffee, but due to its distinct taste, it is better used as a coffee blend to add complexity and depth of flavor. Originating in Liberia, West Africa, Liberica has spread to parts of Southeast Asia such as the Philippines, Indonesia, Malaysia, and Vietnam.

The Philippines was the first country to cultivate Liberica, establishing it as a significant coffee culture. Despite Arabica being more popular, Liberica maintains a stable position in the Asian-Pacific market. The coffee industry in the Philippines has made efforts to preserve the remaining Liberica cultivation areas from extinction, resulting in improved agricultural practices and increased coffee production.

When the Philippines gained independence, it led to a decline in Liberica coffee on the global market as the production began to degrade.

In Malaysia and the Philippines, Liberica is not as rare. Liberica coffee is well-known in the Philippines as well as significant in Malaysia. While Arabica remains the most consumed coffee, Liberica still maintains a stable position in the Asia-Pacific market, unlike the global market.

The coffee industry in the Philippines has endeavored to preserve the remaining areas cultivated with Liberica from extinction. Additionally, both the government and private sector have made efforts and achieved successful improvements in acceptable agricultural practices. This effort has resulted in an increase in the availability of sufficient beans and a continuous growth in coffee production.

Malaysia also produces a significant amount of Liberica coffee. However, it is not as significant for global production. The main types of coffee planted in this country are Liberica and Robusta, constituting around 73% and 27% of coffee production in the country, making them the primary coffee varieties.

Liberica cannot produce significant yields that could sustain the global demand for coffee. The global demand is substantially higher than the local supply. Besides being grown in a few countries, its global production is limited to small quantities.

One of the reasons for this is that people are not really engaging in research today. Liberica is often mixed with other varieties like Robusta just to be sold in the market, as sometimes, even locally, there is no demand for it.

Liberica coffee is often defined as a plant of tropical plains. This coffee plant thrives in low altitudes (up to 600 meters) as Liberica performs better in such environments than Arabica, and even Robusta.

Liberica coffee clusters are the largest among coffee varieties. Sometimes the size can vary as well. The most elongated bean, that's for sure.

The taste of Liberica coffee may differ slightly from what you commonly drink. But what distinguishes the taste of Liberica coffee from any other is its fruitiness.

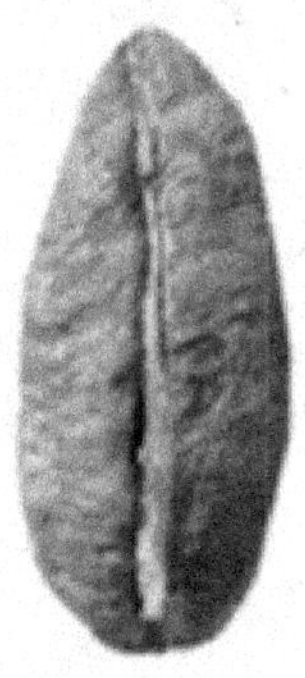

Liberica bean.[8]

BARISTA

A barista is a hospitality professional who excels in the preparation of espresso-based drinks, utilizing various blends of espresso. In other words, they create a variety of coffee beverages using espresso as a base with additional ingredients.

They possess extensive knowledge of coffee as a foundation and all the variations that can be derived from it, understand the coffee they work with, and the machine they operate, and are passionate about crafting artistic creations from espresso, milk, and additives.

The speed at which a barista works is astounding, perhaps even faster than a bartender.

A professional barista will identify machine issues before a technician arrives, perform calibration to adjust the grinder for the perfect espresso dose and grind size, ensuring a quality espresso they can take pride in.

They never wait for a technician to tune the grinder, making adjustments much more frequently, even daily. Similarly, a barista doesn't wait for a monthly deep clean of the machine; they have the tools, like a "blind filter," and follow the manufacturer's instructions diligently. Don't be surprised if they do this every evening and expect the same from colleagues, whom they ensure are trained correctly in the process. Proper training is necessary due to the use of chemical products.

You may observe them attentively listening to the machine while cleaning, observing the water flow, repeating the process until satisfied, and meticulously cleaning the head above the handle with a brush. Witnessing such dedication is beautiful. My recommendation is to do this every evening.

Espresso machine handle without machine sieve.[9]

In the image above, you can see a so-called portafilter handle, a handle into which an espresso coffee filter is placed. The handle is shown after washing and cleaning, meaning it is ready to receive the also washed filter and produce high-quality espresso beverages.

It is easiest to wash by soaking it for 10-15 minutes in a diluted espresso machine cleaning solution and vigorously scrubbing it with a coarse cloth or a tool designed for that purpose. It is important not to use rough tools to remove residue from the handles so as not to damage the surface through which coffee flows to the cup after passing through the filter.

This is not a process that needs to be done daily but once a week is sufficient. However, I recommend doing it every evening with machine cleaning as it will be easier to maintain the hygiene of the handles rather than waiting for 7 days. Cleaning the handle is physically easier and takes minimal time.

The importance of the cleanliness of this handle lies in the fact that over time, a lot of coffee residue builds up. This residue is accumulated due to the temperature of the machine head, which affects the handle.

The temperature of this handle in the machine is 95°C, which facilitates the sticking of the residue. Accumulated coffee and residue that continues to flow with each new espresso you pour affects the taste of the new espresso in the cup. The residue stuck in the handle becomes bitter and starts transferring a bad taste to the subsequent coffees you make.

For this reason, the hygiene of the handles, as well as the machine and filters placed in the handle, is important.

A sieve for one dose of espresso coffee.[10]

A sieve for two doses of espresso coffee.[11]

Above are shown sieves for one and two doses of espresso coffee. From the image itself, it can be seen that for a double dose, the volume of the sieve is double, which is logical, but the handles they attach to are different.

The larger sieve goes on a handle with two spouts/faucets located on the lower side of the handle through which the coffee flows. For a single dose, there is a handle with a single spout/faucet underneath, and it is important not to mix them when assembling the sieve and handles after washing.

Hygiene of the sieves in which coffee is dosed from the espresso grinder is as important as other parts. The residue also accumulates easily, especially due to the aforementioned temperature of 95 C.

Sieves are vessels in which espresso coffee is dosed before releasing the machine to pour coffee. The word "sieve" itself indicates that the construction of the bottom of the vessel is perforated, and over time, the fine holes get dirty and simply clog to the point where the sieve gets blocked; hardly any coffee can pass through.

The easiest way to check is by removing/detaching the sieve from the handle, rinsing it under a water stream, then directing it towards brightness and looking through the sieve. It will show which holes are blocked, i.e., to what extent the sieve is dirty and clogged.

Cleaning is easiest with a rough sponge and a little powder for washing espresso machines. Preventatively, it is best to soak the sieves once a week along with the handles for weekly cleaning and simply clean and wash them when washing the handles, as mentioned earlier. This way, you get a nice and clean unit when you connect the sieves with the handles.

It is preferable to discard and write to the waste the first coffees after these washings.

Blind sieve for washing appliances.[12]

The blind sieve is used to clean the espresso machine itself, i.e. the system of pipes in the espresso machine through which the coffee is obtained, i.e. the hot water from the boiler where the water is heated and pressure is achieved but we will talk about that in subsequent lines. Now, let's focus on cleaning the machine itself using the blind sieve.

The blind sieve is called that because it has no holes in it. Every evening, the blind sieve/filter should be placed in the handle and then a certain amount of machine cleaning powder should be poured into it.

It is a small amount of powder and it is best to follow the instructions of the manufacturer of the cleaning chemical/powder you are using.

After that, the handle with the blind sieve/filter and powder is placed in the espresso machine head and the machine is allowed to run as if making coffee for a certain number of seconds, then turned off and the process is repeated five-ten times. After that, you turn it on again the same way, but each time you pour out the contents from the blind sieve/filter. You repeat this process until no more foam comes out of the exhaust pipes above the espresso machine drain/grid.

Clean water must start flowing to make sure you have removed all the chemicals from that part of the system and then move on to cleaning the other group's machine head and other parts of the system.

The group machine heads also need to be cleaned and there are special brushes for that. Simply clean the inside of the espresso machine head and then turn it on to let a little water run through and rinse the cleaning brush. Repeat the process until you no longer see any coffee residue on the brush.

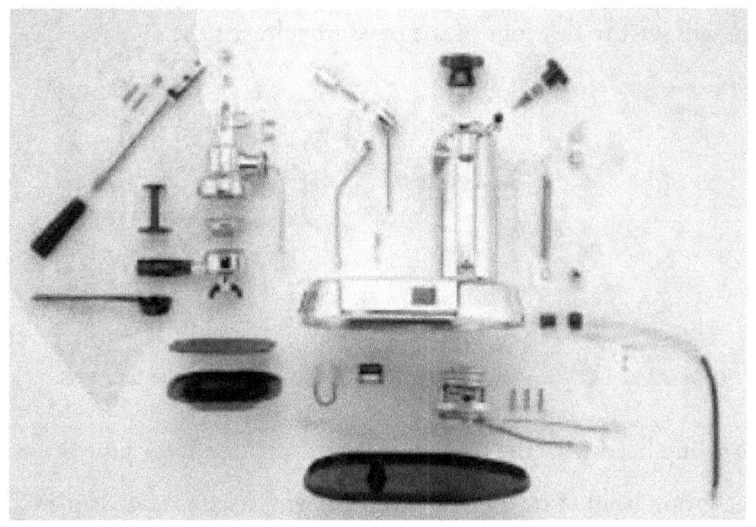

The espresso machine group head.[13]

The machine cleaning process should be done every evening before closing the premises or after closing, depending on the rules of the cafeteria and the company that owns the cafeteria. It should be described in the company's SOP (Standard Operational Procedures).

The first coffee should be poured/thrown out in the morning and recorded as waste. This is done to ensure the removal of any possible leftover chemicals and to allow the coffee flavor to pass through the system and handles. This also enhances the quality of the first coffees by preventing a lack of aroma.

The group head of the machine is where the handle is placed when making coffee. Each machine group head is cleaned from within, and each has a back pressure release tube for excess water and pressure. It is noticeable in the background of the machine's group head, which has a grid where you place the cup to pour/extract the coffee. You will easily spot it when cleaning the machine if you haven't done so before, as foam from the cleaning chemical will come out of it.

The foam starts when, for example, after using the blind filter, you start pouring/extracting for a few seconds, and when you turn it off, the foam will start to flow out of the pressure release tube.

The group head with the handle. The pressure discharge pipe between the group head of the device and the device itself is also visible.[14] Pouring coffee from the machine into an espresso cup after pressing a button is called **coffee extraction**.

From household espresso machines with one group head to traditional ones with 2 group heads in cafes, you will also come across espresso machines with 3 or more group heads in busier and larger cafes. In such cafes, you may notice multiple espresso coffee machines.

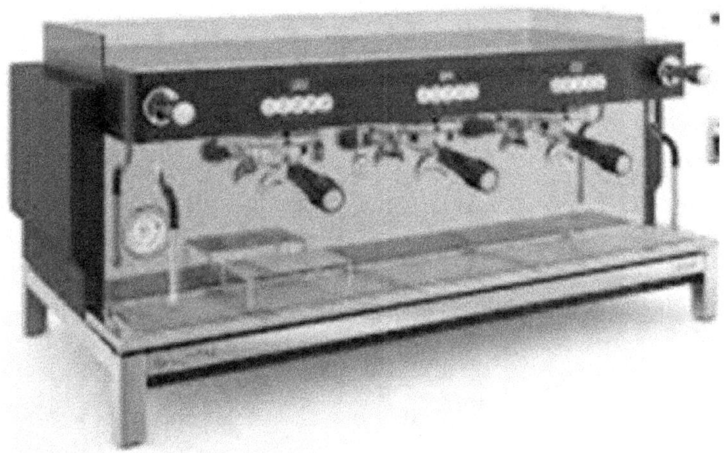

Espresso machine with three group heads.[15]

Washing the espresso machine with a powder intended for that use.[16]

One of the many chemical agents in powder form for washing espresso machines.[17]

HEATING OF CUPS AND THE TEMPERATURE NEEDED FOR SERVING

Baristas leave cups on the espresso machine for several reasons, all crucial to ensuring the quality of the coffee they serve guests.

One of the primary reasons is to have the cups dry and warm, even hot. A warmer cup reduces the possibility and danger of contamination, decreasing the chance of harmful bacteria developing.

Warm cups help maintain the espresso's temperature when extracted/poured, preventing it from cooling too quickly. This is particularly important because serving espresso in a cold cup can impact the taste.

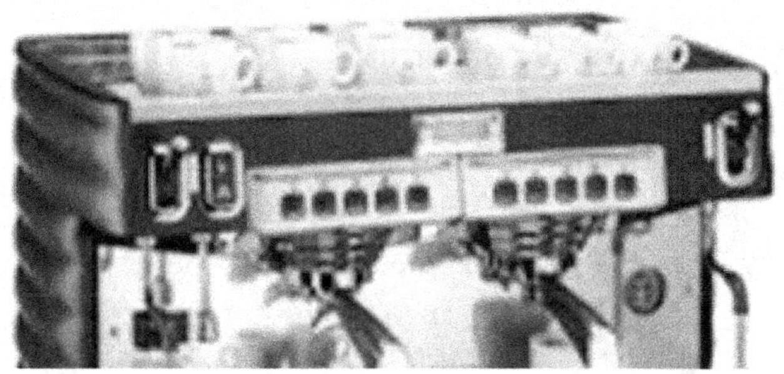

Heating cups on the espresso machine.[18]

Preheating the cups beforehand ensures that the coffee stays at the optimal temperature for longer, preserving its flavor and aroma.

Cold cups can quickly cool down espresso, resulting in a less pleasant drinking experience, the opposite of what is desired.

By preheating the cups on the espresso machine, baristas can guarantee that the coffee remains at the perfect temperature from the first to the last sip. Additionally, by keeping the cups on the espresso machine, baristas ensure that any residual moisture or impurities are evaporated or removed.

Moist cups can dilute the coffee and alter its flavor profile, something baristas want to avoid. Therefore, by keeping the cups dry, baristas can maintain the integrity of the coffee and deliver a consistent, high-quality product to their guests.

Overall, the practice of leaving the cups on the espresso machine is a simple yet essential step in the coffee-making process that contributes to the overall quality and consistency of the final product.

By keeping the cups dry, warm, and preheated, baristas can ensure that every cup of coffee they serve meets the highest standards and provides guests with a delightful and satisfying coffee experience.

Standard is a key element and role of a coffee shop, especially for regular customers.

Heating larger cups such as those for lattes is easiest on the espresso machine's steamer. Releasing steam into the cup for a few seconds achieves the desired result, a hot cup.

Another way to heat the large cup is to pour a little hot water into it and let it sit while you heat the milk in the latte pitcher/jug and on the other side pour the espresso shot for latte coffee. Then, once you have everything prepared, pour out the hot water from the large cup, and the cup will automatically dry and become hot. Of course, for heating, pour approximately 30-50ml of hot water at the bottom of the cup. A larger quantity is not necessary and can even be harmful because the cup might remain wet when you start preparing the drink in it.

MAINTAINING HYGIENE OF COFFEE CUPS AND GLASSES

27

Coffee contains a certain amount of oil and foam, and since it is usually served hot, it leaves traces on the cup more easily than on a regular glass, requiring more effort to clean. Lipstick stains are also often found, so special attention should be paid to the hygiene of coffee cups.

Simply putting the cup in the dishwasher is often not enough; it must be rinsed by hand first to remove lipstick and stubborn residue. Sugar also tends to stick quite firmly to the bottom of the cup even though the guest may stir the coffee after adding sugar.

No matter how much effort you put into washing and maintaining the cups clean, I recommend soaking them in a solution of water and espresso machine cleaner twice a month. Any remaining dirt is easiest to notice at the bottom of the cup or on the handle-cup junction. It is very important to thoroughly rinse the cups after using aggressive chemicals to avoid any undesired effects.

Residues of chemicals can be harmful.

PREPARING COFFEE

Espresso coffee is a blend of Arabica, Robusta, and Liberica coffee beans. Most blends are made from Arabica and Robusta beans.

The most expensive coffee in the world is Kopi Luwak. The secret lies in the coffee beans passing through the digestive system of the Civet animal before being collected and processed.

The prices of a cup of this coffee are exorbitant.

Civet, the animal that "helps" in obtaining Kopi Luwak coffee.[19]

Packaging of the most expensive coffee in the world, Kopi Luwak.[20]
In various hospitality magazines, textbooks, and the like, you will come
across explanations about coffee, its names, appearances, and
preparation methods. Explanations about espresso machines, grinders,
refrigerators, and everything necessary for a coffee shop.

Different coffee distributors may even offer training sessions.

In principle, all of this is quite similar and looks the same. It may
seem so to people who are not deeply involved in the profession.

Working in a well-known global chain of coffee shops can earn
you the title of a coffee maestro, which is not easy to achieve. In
Montenegro, only two individuals held this title for such a company:
they wore silver coffee beans as a badge on their shirt collars. Their
task was to provide training and assistants who could deliver quality
training so that, for example, a traveler drinking coffee in Tivat at the
airport or in Podgorica would have the same experience as in a coffee
shop of the same chain in Belgrade, London, Milan, Dubai, etc.

Ensuring that coffee is prepared in the same way, that milk is
steamed/heated with thermometers in pitchers at temperatures
specified by standards. The grinder was calibrated three times a day, and

this was recorded in a daily log, as were the refrigerator temperatures. Humidity in the air and various factors can affect how coffee is extracted throughout the day, not to mention from day to day. Often little importance is given to this, or rather little importance is attached, and as long as the "master" sets it up, that's it. No employee is allowed to touch it. This is not the correct or proper way of thinking.

There is a significant difference in how coffee is impacted, for instance, in a coastal cafe on a hot sunny day as opposed to a rainy day with high humidity in the air. Coffee is one of the 7 groceries with the greatest ability to absorb external influences in the world.

For this reason, I will briefly share here from my practice what others have taught me as the standard in the company, whose name I do not mention for advertisement purposes.

I have often encountered different opinions from people who are passionate about espresso machines, but I have remained loyal to the school I have attended. This school, which taught me the art of making various espresso coffee drinks, appealed to me the most. Everything I did afterward only made me more confident in my positive opinion of that school.

One thing I would like to emphasize is that I never put a spoon in the milk pitcher or use it in the preparation of coffee drinks. Using a spoon is a habit from older generations of baristas, and for many, it helps achieve certain results without the need. Once you get used to working without a spoon in making a Cappuccino, for example, you will never use it again for any coffee, except when drinking it, perhaps.

Steaming milk to create different types of foam for various drinks can be a nightmare for beginners and seems like something to give up on.

Beginners often think they will never master it, but they are mistaken. Many have become convinced of this. Training is necessary for everything you want to do successfully. Persistent work and training in the right way with an adequate trainer yield secure results.

Espresso coffee, Classic Espresso

Espresso coffee is 30ml of espresso extracted into a small, hot espresso cup. The extraction duration should be 20 seconds. You will get the most beautiful coffee foam when the coffee drips down the walls of the cup.

If you have time, I recommend lifting the cup slightly and controlling the flow down the cup's wall. The foam should be thick and from where it dripped in the cup, spreading the foam's color in layers.

30ml of espresso in making other coffees and in recipe writing is commonly referred to as a **shot.**

Espresso coffee classic.[21]

Americano coffee

Americanos are made in various ways, with people demonstrating creativity with water.

Americano is actually most similar to filter coffee, which is the most commonly consumed coffee in America.

Pour hot water from an espresso machine into a hot cappuccino cup, leaving room for 30ml of espresso. Gently release a stream of espresso coffee along the cup's wall, allowing a beautiful coffee foam to form on the water's surface.

The result is Americano coffee.

Espresso Americano.[22]

Macchiato coffee

Espresso coffee with milk in a hot small espresso cup.

Macchiato got its name from the Italian word macchia, which means a spot.

Therefore, it means that it is wrong to make a mini cappuccino out of macchiato, but as already mentioned: espresso coffee (30ml) with a little milk and a white dot on the coffee foam.

You will get the dot by using a bit of milk foam that you will surely get by heating the milk. Sometimes, a guest might ask for a macchiato with cold milk.

In that case, it should be served exclusively with cold milk because the taste is different compared to coffee with hot milk.

Espresso macchiato.[23]

Latte Coffee

It is a milky mild coffee.

The most beautiful way to serve it is in a tall glass with a handle that tapers at the bottom. It is good to serve it with a long "neck" spoon or a HACCP-approved straw for hot milk. If you serve it with the mentioned straw, the long "neck" spoon is not necessary. The straw can be used to mix sugar.

Prepare it by pouring heated milk into a warm glass and adding 1 to 1.5cm of milk foam, then pour a shot of coffee on top in the middle to create a point in the center of the foam. This is the reason for recommending serving this coffee in a glass, and the magical color transition that takes place before the eyes of the observer.

Espresso latte coffee.[24]

Ice Latte Coffee

It's a milky and cold coffee.

It's best served in a tall glass with a handle that tapers at the bottom.

It's good to serve it with a spoon with a long "neck" or a straw. If serving with a straw, the spoon with a long "neck" is not necessary.

The difference between Ice Latte Coffee and Latte Coffee is in the temperature of the milk because Ice Latte Coffee is made with cold milk poured over ice cubes that are previously placed in a chilled glass, followed by cold foam that is easily made, even by hand.

Finally, a shot of espresso is poured over, beautifully settling and spreading down the ice cubes, creating a lovely image as it mixes with the milk.

Espresso Ice Latte coffee.[25]

Cappuccino

It was named after Italian monks from the Capuchin order.

Stronger than a Caffe Latte, it is made with thick milk foam. Typically, a cappuccino should consist of one-third coffee, one-third milk, and one-third foam.

It is most beautiful when you manage to create a cappuccino so that during serving, there is a prominent circle of coffee color with coffee foam around the cappuccino foam along the edge of the cup.

Cappuccino coffee.[26]

Ice coffee

- The first recipe is the same procedure and recipe as with Latte coffee, except you pour cold milk over a full glass of ice, leaving room for 1-1.5cm of foam and a shot of espresso on top in the middle. This creates an even more beautiful sight than with a classic latte because of the ice in the glass. It has already been described above as Ice Latte. Here, we are talking about a recipe from one company. I prefer to call this coffee Ice Latte the most.

- The second recipe is milk with a scoop of ice cream and a shot of espresso on top.

- The third recipe is milk with a scoop of ice cream, a shot of espresso, and whipped cream on top. I recommend this as a true Ice coffee, but always explain the coffee content to the guest.

- The fourth recipe is instant coffee, milk, a scoop of ice cream, and a shot of espresso.

These were the Ice coffee recipes I encountered.

Coffee fredo

Often confused in preparation with ice coffee, it's actually a long shot of espresso poured over crushed ice and a little water. Pour a little water, crushed ice, and a long shot of espresso. Simply put, an Iced Americano. The name comes from the Italian word "fredo," meaning cold.

Coffee Fredo.[27]

Mocha coffee

Mocha is a coffee that is prepared similarly to cappuccino, but it requires choosing the right cocoa to add to the milk when making the foam.

It's not easy to choose the right cocoa because most cocoa breaks down and ruins the foam you create for a cappuccino. Therefore, you need to put in some effort and experiment until you achieve the desired result.

Many make mocha with hot chocolate, which, in my opinion, is not a true mocha. Although, I must admit it is delicious, but I would rather call it coffee with hot chocolate.

Moccha coffee.[28]

Desert Crema Coffee

Coffee manufacturers have come up with the idea of creating a dessert that resembles ice cream for hot days but has the taste of coffee.

Initially prepared by hand, machines for cold dessert Crema Coffee were eventually developed. These machines are similar to ice cream makers.

This coffee is properly prepared by mixing sweet cream, espresso coffee, sugar, and some additional ingredients such as hazelnut or other flavors. Manufacturers often selfishly guard their recipes for generations. It is vigorously mixed and left to cool until it thickens.

In today's world, coffee manufacturers offer a powder blend with the necessary ingredients to which the required milliliters of espresso coffee and milk are added, then vigorously stirred, and the mixture is poured into the cold dessert Crema Coffee machine.

Crema coffee machine.[29]

DECAF COFFEE

Decaf coffee is intended for individuals who are allergic to caffeine or simply do not tolerate it well but still enjoy the taste of coffee.

Decaf coffee is not obtained in traditional bags or sacks, instead, each dose is packaged in its sachet and mesh, similar to tea bags. It is round in shape and flat. The dose is placed in the sieve/filter handle for decaf coffee, and the machine head group should be lightly cleaned beforehand. The easiest way is to let a little water pass through the machine head group, clean it with a brush, and then let a little water pass again before placing the handle with decaf coffee for caffeine-free coffee extraction.

Cafeterias have a separate handle for decaf coffee, with its sieve/filter handle, and that handle is kept separate from the machine. It usually has a red handle to emphasize its purpose, as allergies should not be risked.

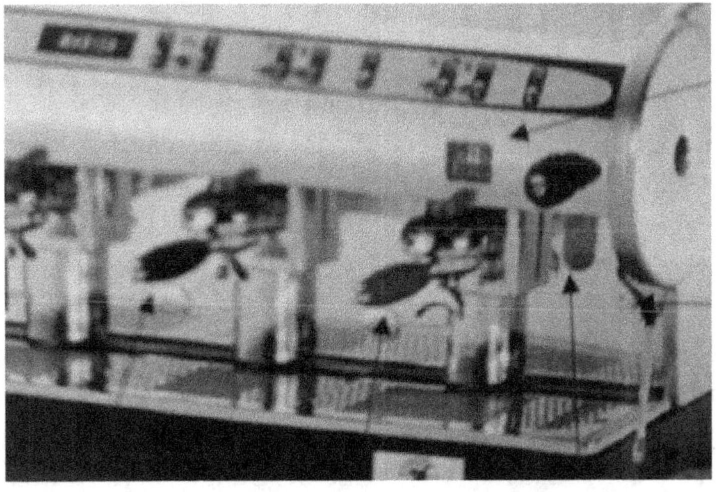

Red handle for decaffeinated coffee according to the textbook of the world-famous chain of cafeterias.

PROCESSES FOR OBTAINING AND PRODUCING DECAFFEINATED COFFEE

Decaffeinated coffee can be obtained through various methods, each aimed at removing caffeine from coffee beans while preserving the flavor as much as possible.

The most well-known methods are:

- The water processing method uses water as a solvent to remove caffeine from green coffee beans. A mixture of water and green coffee extract circulates around the beans. The caffeine-rich extract will then pass through activated charcoal, which absorbs the caffeine.

- The direct solvent method involves softening the beans through soaking or steaming, then rinsing them multiple times with a chemical solvent like ethyl acetate or methylene chloride to eliminate caffeine. The solvent is then evaporated, and the beans are washed with water to remove any remaining residue of the solvent.

- The indirect solvent process entails soaking the beans in hot water, which is then treated with a chemical solvent once it becomes caffeine-rich. The resulting decaffeinated water is reintroduced to the beans, allowing them to reabsorb some of the flavors.

- The supercritical carbon dioxide method uses CO_2 under high pressure and temperature to extract caffeine without significantly affecting the taste of coffee.

- The Swiss water process involves soaking the beans in hot water to extract caffeine and flavors without chemicals. The water is then passed through a charcoal filter to remove caffeine. Flavor-rich water is used to rinse the next batch of beans, ensuring the aromas stay within the beans. This process is most similar to the first method described.

INSTANT COFFEE

1771. The first "instant coffee" was created in Britain. It was called a "coffee component," and the British government patented it.

1853. The first American instant coffee product was produced during the Civil War. Soldiers received an experimental type of instant coffee.

1901. A Japanese chemist, Dr. Sartori Kato in Chicago, Illinois, developed the first successful method for preparing stable soluble coffee powder, known as instant coffee. The name "instant" comes from the simple process of making the drink: mix coffee powder with water, and there you have your desired beverage. Dr. Kato was already known for developing techniques for making instant tea, which he then applied to coffee. In 1903, he obtained a patent for his method.

1909. Mass production of instant coffee began for the first time. An American inventor who emigrated from Belgium did this in America.

George K.L. Washington (1871-1946) created instant coffee products after seeing coffee powder around the edge of a silver coffee pot during his stay in Guatemala.

Although Washington obtained a patent for what would become the first mass-produced instant coffee, it was considered to have a rather unsatisfactory taste. He named it "Red E Coffee" and began selling it in 1909.

1914-1918. Instant coffee became popular, especially among the American military, which bought all available supplies. During World War I, soldiers referred to it as "George's Cup." Even when the army returned home, the desire for the product did not diminish, and consumption of instant coffee continued.

1930. The Brazilian Coffee Institute asked the President of Nestle to create a soluble coffee product with an acceptable coffee taste (e.g., "instant coffee") to help Brazil deal with its abundant surplus of coffee and potentially increase overall coffee sales. Nestle then embarked on several years of intensive research to address these issues.

Scientist Max Morgenthaler of the "Nestle" company developed a new technique for making instant coffee at the "Nestle Research Center" laboratory in Switzerland in 1937. The latest product, "Nescafe," comes from combining "Nestle" and "Cafe" productions.

"Nestle" began selling "Nescafe" in Switzerland on April 1, 1938, and also started producing it in their factory in London in 1938. Their new instant coffee process involves drying equal amounts of coffee extract and soluble carbohydrates, producing better-tasting instant coffee that quickly became a popular product. The American army became the main buyer.

From 1939 to 1945, during World War II, instant coffee was very popular among soldiers. "Nescafe" and other instant coffee brands delivered large quantities to the growing market. During one year of the war, the American army bought more than a million boxes of "Nescafe." This was the entire annual production of the "Nestle" factory in the US.

In 1943, George Washington's company was sold to "American Home Products" just before Washington's death. The George Washington coffee brand continued until 1961, but "George Washington Seasoning & Broth" is still sold today.

In 1950, coffee was the favorite drink of teenagers listening to rock and roll in cafes.

In 1954, "Nescafe" developed a method for producing instant coffee using only coffee, with the previous addition of carbohydrates for stabilization. The following year, they introduced "Nescafe Blend 37."

In 1960, an improved-looking instant coffee was developed using a process called "aggregation," which involved steaming instant coffee particles to clump together. Unfortunately, the heating/drying cycle affected the taste of the coffee, so the method was improved. Freezing drying became the desirable method for making instant coffee.

In 1961, "Nestle" introduced a new era in corporate design with its iconic jars.

In 1970, "Nestle" began selling its instant coffee in transparent glass jars.

Nes instant coffee is usually made with hot milk. A small amount of liquid is poured into the bottom of the container, then the necessary dose of coffee is added, and it is mixed with a special machine. This process produces the valued coffee foam, to which hot milk is then added and served. Many cafes have their type of decoration with chocolate or similar, depending on the company's rules, although it is correct to serve it without any additions, except for sugar on the side. It is served in a tall glass, usually with a handle into which a straw and a long spoon are added. You will often see Nes coffee served without a spoon, which is not correct, as many guests enjoy the coffee foam, especially if ordered with whipped cream.

A guest can request Nes coffee made only with water or without foam, as well as cold Nes coffee or Nes coffee with whipped cream.

Various additives can be given to Nes instant coffee, as mentioned in the section on additives for espresso, cappuccino, latte, etc.

Instant coffee can also be poured into automatic coffee machines. This is most commonly seen in offices around the world. Of course, there are also household versions of these machines.

Vending machines commonly have labels with pre-made products as the options you want. Nowadays, even images of the products themselves are displayed. With just a touch of a button, you get your desired, favorite coffee.

Ness instant coffee in boxes and cans.[30]

Ness instant coffee in a glass that succeeded cans.[31]

Gold Blend Nes instant coffee.[32]

Decaf Nes instant coffee without caffeine.[33]

A sachet with a dose of Ness instant coffee, which caterers are
increasingly using.[34]

These sachets have become beloved as they provide the precise
necessary dose for one coffee, and also greatly facilitate control of the
quantity during inventory and orders. Another advantage is that a
single-dose sachet always promises freshness, unlike an open box,
especially if the box has been sitting for a long time.

Nes kafa.[35]

Nes instant coffee with whipped cream.[36]

Machines for preparing Ness coffee in cafeterias.

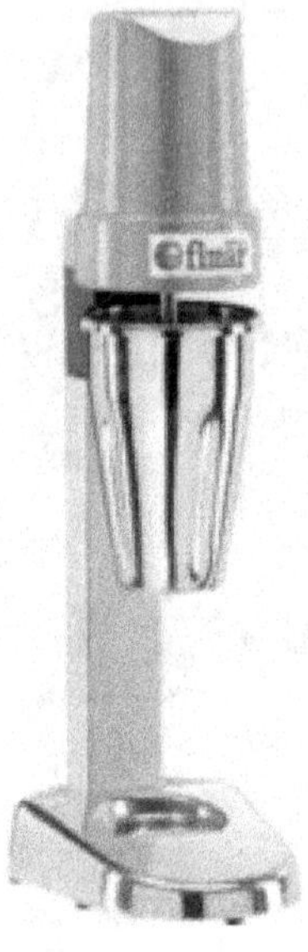

Machines for preparing Ness coffee in cafeterias.[37]

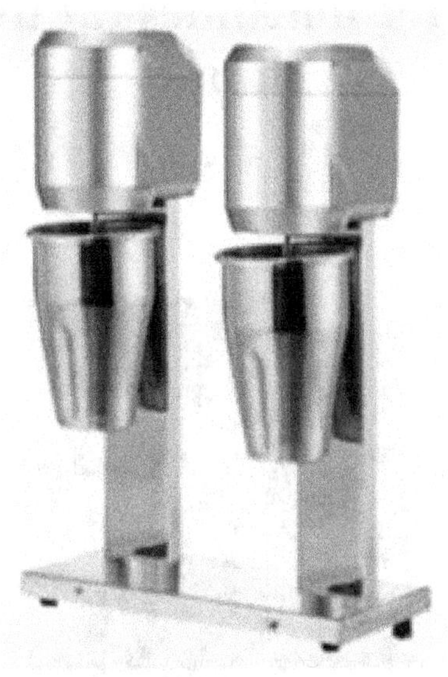

Professional double Nes coffee machine.[38]

Instant coffee machines for the office and home.

Automatic instant coffee machine.[39]

Instant coffee machine.[40]

DEVICES FOR MAKING FOAM WITHOUT STEAMERS

To make cold foam, it is logical that you cannot do it on an espresso machine. You can still find small milk frothers for getting cold foam in cafes, even when not in use, they serve as decoration for the cafe.

The traditional way of "beating" milk is to obtain cold foam.[41] The traditional milk frothing device consists of a pitcher with a lid and a plunger that has a mesh at the bottom as a strainer, allowing the barista to vigorously move the milk up and down to create foam.

Nowadays, electric frothers are used, which have the option to adjust for hot or cold foam, making the barista's job easier, although losing the charming feeling of tradition.

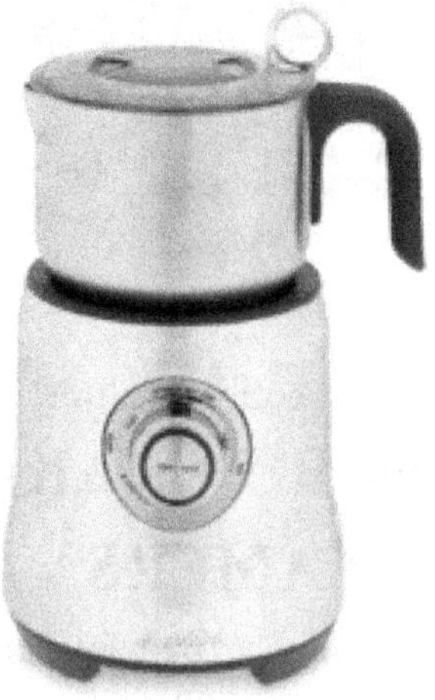

A modern electric device that makes cold or hot foam depending on Commands.[42]

ESPRESSO COFFEE GRINDER

The espresso coffee grinder is one of the most important items in a coffee shop. It carries equal importance as the coffee machine itself. The only difference is that it is easier to have a spare grinder physically and replace it in case of a malfunction until it is repaired.

The grinder consists of a hopper for whole coffee beans, a container for ground coffee, a calibration system, and a handle or button for dosing. Nowadays, digital grinders are mostly in use, which have a dosing button with a display.

The mentioned grinding system consists of two commonly brass circular blades with toothed edges, and these sharp teeth are facing each other. They rotate in opposite directions. Coffee beans from the hopper fall between these two gears, and a fine powder for making espresso coffee comes out of them.

The calibration system consists of a component that adjusts the gap between the grinding gears to determine the coarseness of the coffee bean grinding.

This ensures the correct granularity of the ground coffee needed for a quality espresso.

The second step for calibration is leveling the coffee grinder doser, located in the ground coffee silo, to determine how much ground coffee will "drop" when the espresso dose handle is pressed/pulled or a button.

Calibrating the coffee grinder is done by adjusting these two systems so that you get 30 ml of espresso coffee in measuring jugs in 20 seconds.

This is usually done with a double dose, placing two measuring jugs under the double dose handle. Before that, of course, the handle is filled with two doses of ground coffee from the grinder, properly tamped, and placed in the machine head group, and coffee is allowed to flow and extract espresso into the two mentioned measuring jugs. When the espresso starts flowing, the stopwatch is started, and in 20 seconds, 2x 30 ml should fill the 2 jugs.

Coffee that is ground too finely will make the coffee flow slower and heavier, requiring more time, while coffee that is ground too coarse will flow too quickly and produce weak coffee. Water will literally "run through" coffee grounds too coarsely.

The other calibration factor, the doser, will determine the amount of coffee and the weight which, if too much, will slow the coffee down, whereas a small dose will result in water passing too quickly, producing a "fast" coffee.

For these reasons, the best calibration is using a stopwatch and measuring jugs. Of course, experience and training are necessary, which are a normal part of the job for baristas, while in small independent cafes or restaurants, managers or owners will call a technician when they see something is wrong with the coffee. Coffee can change its characteristics 2-3 times a day depending on the weather conditions, especially if it's a seaside cafe, for example. That is why the knowledge and routine carried out by baristas are important.

"Slow" coffee will taste bitter, astringent and burnt.

"Fast" coffee will be weak with a lack of aroma, taste and smell.

Various grinders for espresso coffee.[43]

MALI ESPRESSO MACHINES FOR HOME OR OFFICE

Caffeine is what many people need to start their day. Some consider it a dependency and a bad habit, even unhealthy, but the fact is that an incredible percentage of the world's population's first move upon waking up is to make themselves coffee. And then at work, another one to kick off the day at least.

Nowadays, all of this is made easier with numerous small espresso machines for home and office use. They are even being perfected to be as close as possible, in terms of features, to professional ones, extracting quality espresso with quality foam, having a steamer that works like on a professional machine, a cup heating space, and most importantly, taking up as little space as possible in the area we inhabit. This has led to a new market for espresso coffee and equipment.

We witness significant innovations daily. Let's not forget that all small machines are still small machines and, in my opinion, they lack sufficient pressure, a strong enough steamer, temperature maintenance, cup heating, and the final product.

Espresso machine for home and office use.[44]

Home espresso machine.[45]

An old household pot for preparing espresso coffee. You can often find it on sale even now, and in cafeterias as a nice souvenir.[46]

PROPER TAMPERING OF COFFEE AND WHY IT IS IMPORTANT

Tamping coffee, or more precisely, applying pressure to the coffee in the portafilter, is a crucial step in the espresso-making process involving compressing the coffee in the portafilter handle before brewing/thermal processing. The thermal processing temperature is 95°C.

The purpose of tamping coffee: Tamping coffee is done to ensure that the coffee dose is evenly distributed by hand and to create a uniform surface through which water can pass during the brewing/thermal processing process. Proper tamping helps control the water flow through the coffee dose, resulting in a more balanced extraction and a better espresso taste.

Baristas typically apply a tamping pressure of around 12 kg of force, although this can vary depending on the coffee blend and personal preferences. I have most commonly encountered a proper pressure of 12-13kg.

Maintaining a constant pressure and tamping technique is key to achieving quality and standard-compliant espresso. Baristas often practice and refine their tamping technique to ensure repeatable results. All this is aimed at achieving a consistent standard that keeps customers coming back.

Tamping affects the quality of espresso by influencing the extraction process. Over-tamping can lead to slow extraction and a bitter taste, while under-tamping can result in a quick liquid flow and a sour taste, even without flavor and aroma.

The quality of the tamper used can also affect the tamping process. High-quality tampers will assist baristas in achieving more consistent and precise tamping. A flat surface is the solution.

Keep the tamper level and evenly press the coffee dose for 2 to 3 seconds.

Gently rotate the tamper during tamping to ensure an even distribution of the coffee dose if you are not using an automatic tamper with a mechanism.

Practice tamping to improve your technique over time. Drink coffee, as it adds to the experience.

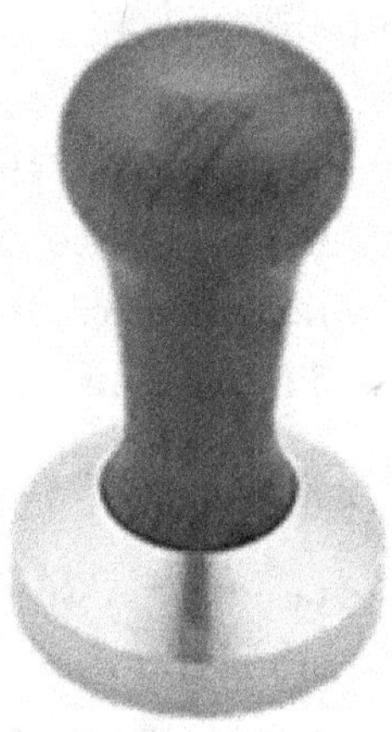

Handle for correct coffee compression. Tamper.[47]

Pressing espresso coffee into a sieve.[48]

Experts have also made an effort to create a system that facilitates the job for baristas and enables constant equal pressure for tamping.

Below is a set for baristas that includes a rubber mat placed on the work surface where you will find a Leveler and a Tamper with automatically adjusted pressing force and limit.

Barista tools: a rubber base for work, a Leveler on the right which evenly levels the coffee in the portafilter before tamping, and a Tamper on the left with a system that limits and determines the pressure/tamping to a specific weight.

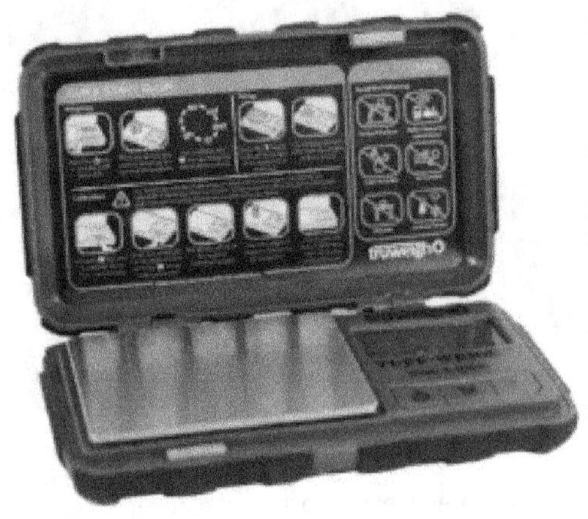

Precision scale for measuring coffee. It is used when controlling coffee doses. It accurately displays the weight of one dose of coffee you are controlling. It is highly precise and shows even parts of a gram, i.e., values lower than 1g (gram).

A FEW WORDS ABOUT STEAMING MILK

Milk frothing, i.e., creating foam through steaming, is often a challenge for bartenders, baristas, and servers, especially beginners in the field.

By heating the milk and positioning the steamer 1.5 cm deep from the surface of the milk along the edge of the pitcher/jug, a circular motion of the milk is created, heating it and transforming it into a light whirlpool. At that moment, the milk begins to form foam and increases in volume. The volume of the milk with foam inside the pitcher increases. It is necessary to lower the pitcher slowly to keep the steamer at 1.5 cm from the surface until the desired results and quality foam are achieved. Care must be taken not to overheat the milk.

Heating the milk above 68 degrees causes it to boil, leading to the loss of foam and the milk boiling over. In such cases, foam cannot be obtained from that milk for a certain period until it cools down, and it is important to note that overheated milk does not have the appropriate taste and aroma of foam as with the first and proper frothing.

For this reason, training improves the process and establishes a routine for the amount of milk frothing for a specific number of servings of desired drinks with as little milk waste as possible. It is important to pay attention, especially at the beginning of training, as injuries can occur due to milk splashing out of the latte cup when it is boiling.

If you only want to heat the milk in the pitcher without foam, submerge the steamer 1.5 cm from the bottom of the pitcher/jug, preferably in the middle without creating a whirlpool. This way, you get hot milk without foam. It is also important to be cautious to prevent overheating of the milk for flavor and taste. Even with this frothing method, the milk can boil over and cause burns if you are not careful and do not follow the necessary procedure.

Skill is acquired through training for various foam variations: more or less foam. Sometimes, a lot of warm milk with little foam is needed.

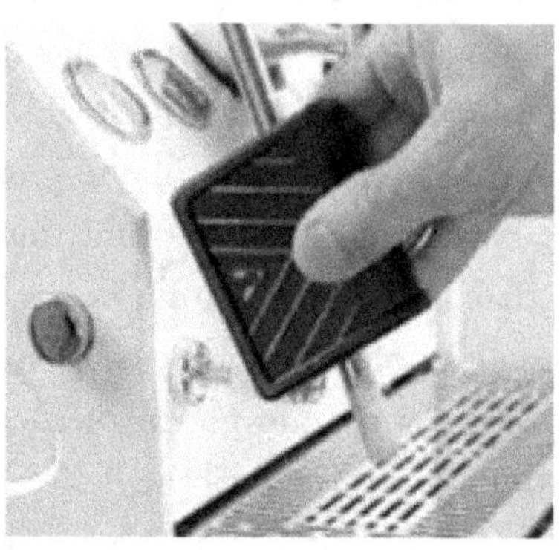

Professional and efficient solution for quickly cleaning steamers during operation. Also, a safe tool to prevent burns and injuries.[49]

The barista never uses a spoon to pour foam from the pitcher/jug into the cup. It's a matter of training. They simply pour it directly from the pitcher into the cup.

A thermometer is what the barista uses while steaming milk in the pitcher/jug for safety and standard. This way, they monitor the milk's exact temperature during the foam's steaming process.

Pitcher / Jug / Latiere with a thermometer.[50]

The thermometer doesn't bother you at all during work once you get used to it and realize how helpful it is. Later, it's hard to work without it. It's excellent for new barista candidates because they can better understand steaming temperatures and limits that need to be managed.

A barista at her workplace with a milk jug and a thermometer.[51]

Digital thermometer for the jug.[52]

Stainless steel/Inox Jug for steaming milk of 1 L.[53]

The Jug 0.75L.[54]

The Jug 0.35L.[55]

There are also smaller stainless steel/inox pitchers than those shown above. They can be 0.2L, 0.15L, and 0.1L, but they require baristas with a lot of experience to work with them. In these, it is easy to overheat the milk, so skill and experience are needed to obtain small amounts of foam if necessary. It's easier to work with larger pitchers than with small ones.

You don't always need to use a milk pitcher of the same volume, but rather depending on the number of drinks you make. If you're making one Cappuccino, you should use a smaller milk pitcher, while for three, you can use a medium or large one. The large pitcher is used for multiple drinks made simultaneously, which usually happens during peak hours.

VARIOUS DRINKS AND INGREDIENTS:

Let's start this title with an example: For instance, a bar, expanding the menu, cocktails. Necessary inventory includes a shaker (I recommend a three-part shaker), Boston shaker, strainer, muddler, bar spoon, various syrups and liqueurs like Cointreau, Triplesec, Kahlua, Malibu coconut rum, Grenadine syrup, Blue curacao, Creme de Cassis, and Angostura bitter. With these few items, along with alcoholic beverages commonly found in most bars, you have 50 cocktails at your fingertips, not to mention if you introduce additional syrups like vanilla, strawberry, raspberry, and so on. A single Mojito can then vary into several different cocktails, with different flavors.

Plant-based milk

Soy milk, coconut milk, almond milk, rice milk... guests may request these, especially vegetarians.

Additionally, individuals with lactose allergies or intolerance, or simply those who enjoy or are accustomed to them, might also indulge in these options. These milks are increasingly used in meal preparation, sauces, desserts, cocktail making, and more.

Coconut milk and pure

Coconut puree and paste are becoming more prevalent in modern hospitality. For example, check out the recipe for the Pina Colada cocktail.

Coconut milk is obtained from grated coconut pulp and grinding the white part of the coconut (meat). It contains fats ranging from 5% to up to 22% depending on the milk's density. It is cholesterol-free.

Tetra Pak coconut milk in the store.[56]

Rice Milk

Rice milk is also a suitable option for individuals who are allergic or intolerant to lactose. Interestingly, even individuals allergic to soy can consume rice milk. It is good to use during fasting days like all plant-based milks, and it is used in both cooking and desserts. It has a low-fat content and does not contain cholesterol.

A tetra pack of rice milk in the store.[57]

Soy milk

Soy milk is made by soaking soybeans, cooking, and straining. The liquid obtained after straining is the milk, and the remaining solids in the cheesecloth can be used to make the popular tofu cheese often mentioned among vegans. Soy milk is most commonly sought after during fasting in our region. It is the most prevalent and cheapest among plant-based milks in our market, and what sets it apart is that it is the easiest to froth for cappuccinos compared to other plant-based milks. It's important to emphasize again that the well-known tofu cheese is derived from soy/soy milk.

Soy milk.[58]

Cocoa

The cocoa tree is a tree not more than 8m tall, whose fruits can weigh up to 0.5kg. They are used for cocoa powder, chocolate production, and cocoa butter. The fruit can also be eaten. It was brought to Europe by Columbus.

Cinnamon

Cinnamon is an aromatic, pleasant spice used in beverages and food. It is delicious and visually appealing, for example, cappuccino sprinkled with cinnamon on top. It is recommended for tea, cornflakes, yogurt, or with more complex dishes. It can be in powder form or grated on the spot.

It is derived from the bark of various cinnamon plants from the same family. Cinnamon families. It is an antioxidant and is beneficial as an addition to the diet for diabetics, a digestive regulator, and useful against respiratory infections. Different cinnamons from this family have different health qualities.

It is important to know that constant use of spices in large quantities can cause unwanted effects and lead to major complications.

Cinnamon.[59]

Toppings

When you mention toppings to a colleague, they will probably first think of coffee with whipped cream and chocolate on top, or a dessert with whipped cream and chocolate or caramel topping, for example. Toppings can be savory or sweet, depending on their use. One restaurant may offer a wide range of toppings, while another may only have one or two.

Toppings are sauces and glazes used for decoration, flavor enhancement, and sometimes as an appetite stimulant. They are used for beverages, appetizers, meals, and desserts. It can be seen as the finishing touch on a finished product, in a nutshell. This gives the impression of completeness to a dessert, for example.

Toppings can be prepared in the restaurant itself, although nowadays most opt for industrially prepared ones. This saves time and costs less.

Toppings of various flavors.[60]

SIRUPI AND LIQUORS FOR ENHANCING FLAVOR

79

MONIN

In the quaint town of Bourges, nestled in the heart of France, there is a small family-owned company that has been creating exquisite syrups for over a century. This is the home of Monin, a name synonymous with quality, flavor, and innovation in the world of syrups.

The story of Monin begins with Georges Monin, a visionary alchemist with a passion for creating unique and delicious flavors. Drawing inspiration from the bountiful orchards and vineyards of the French countryside, Georges set out to capture the essence of fruits, flowers, and herbs in liquid form, crafting syrups that would elevate any beverage to new heights.

One of Monin's most beloved creations is their classic simple syrup, a versatile and essential ingredient in the world of mixology. Made from pure cane sugar and filtered water, this syrup adds a touch of sweetness and balance to cocktails, mocktails, and culinary creations alike, making it a staple in bars and kitchens around the world.

As Monin's reputation grew, so did their range of syrups, expanding to include a vast array of flavors that cater to every palate and preference. From fruity favorites like raspberry and passion fruit to exotic blends like lychee and elderflower, Monin syrups offer endless possibilities for crafting unique and delicious beverages.

In addition to their non-alcoholic syrups, Monin also offers a line of premium liqueur syrups that bring the rich and complex flavors of spirits to cocktails and mocktails without the need for alcohol. Whether you're craving the warmth of bourbon in a classic Old Fashioned or the sweetness of rum in a tropical Daiquiri, Monin's liqueur syrups provide a convenient and delicious way to enjoy your favorite flavors.

Today, Monin syrups are cherished by bartenders, baristas, and home enthusiasts alike, and celebrated for their exceptional quality, consistency, and versatility. With a commitment to sustainability and innovation, Monin continues to push the boundaries of flavor, creating syrups that inspire creativity and delight the senses.

Monin syrups.[61]

De KYPER

In the picturesque town of Schiedam, located in the heart of the Netherlands, there is a distillery with a rich heritage, De Kuiper. It is synonymous with quality and innovation in the world of liqueurs.

The story of De Kuiper dates back to the 17th century when the Dutchman Petrus De Kuiper, a visionary with a passion for distillation and the idea of creating beverages that would captivate the senses and delight the palate, began to develop his ideas. Armed with a deep knowledge of botany and a keen sense of artistry, Petrus created liqueurs that were unlike anything the world had ever seen.

As the word spread about his exceptional creations, De Kuiper's reputation grew, attracting connoisseurs and enthusiasts from afar. The distillery became a center of creativity and experimentation, with each new generation of the De Kuiper family building upon the legacy of their ancestors and pushing the boundaries toward success.

One of De Kuiper's most famous creations is their distinctive cherry liqueur, made from ripe, hand-picked cherries that are macerated to perfection and combined with a secret blend of spices and herbs. The result is a juicy, ruby-red elixir that bursts with the sweet and tangy flavors of sun-ripened fruit. This is a true testament to De Kuiper's dedication to quality and tradition.

Over the centuries, De Kuiper has continued to innovate and evolve, expanding its portfolio to include a wide range of liqueurs, spirits, and cocktail ingredients beloved by bartenders and mixologists around the world. From classic favorites like Triple Sec and Blue Curacao to modern creations such as their innovative range of flavored liqueurs, De Kuiper leads the way in excellence in the spirits industry.

De KYPER liqueurs and syrups.[62]

COFFEE LIQUORS

Kahlua

In the heart of Mexico, where the air is filled with the aroma of roasted coffee beans, lies a small village known for its rich history and vibrant culture. It is in this quaint village that the legend of Kahlua was born.

Locals tell a tale of a mysterious traveler who arrived one fateful night, carrying a small bottle of magical elixir. This elixir, as he claimed, was a blend of the finest Arabica coffee beans, sugarcane, vanilla, and a touch of rum. As he poured the dark, velvety liquid into their cups, the villagers were enchanted by the intoxicating aroma that filled the air.

Each sip enveloped them in warmth and delight, where the bitterness of coffee was perfectly balanced by the sweetness of the liqueur. The traveler, known only as Kahlua, became a beloved figure in the village, sharing his secret recipe with the locals who eagerly embraced this newfound treasure.

Word of the new concoction spread far and wide, attracting travelers from distant lands who yearned to experience the magic of Kahlua for themselves. Soon, the village became a bustling hub of commerce, with merchants selling bottles of the precious elixir to eager customers craving the taste of its incomparable flavor.

Today, Kahlua is enjoyed worldwide, esteemed for its unique blend of coffee and spirits that brings people together in celebration and camaraderie. Whether sipped neat, in cocktails or with a scoop of vanilla ice cream, Kahlua continues to captivate the hearts and palates of all who have the pleasure of indulging in its rich and complex flavors.

Originating in Mexico in 1936, Kahlúa is a coffee liqueur loved worldwide. Used in various drinks—from coffees to cocktails—it goes hand in hand with many occasions. Classic cocktails, like the White Russian, Espresso Martini, and Black Russian just wouldn't be the same without it. With its enticing caramel color, Kahlúa coffee liqueur boasts the deep, rich flavor of real black coffee and indulgent sweet butter.

Alcohol: 12.6%

Kahlua coffee liqueur.[63]

I have mentioned and written about the basic and most commonly used Kahlua liqueur here, which is also produced today with various additives and different flavors.

Sheridans Coffee Layered Liqueur

Sheridans Coffee Layered Liqueur
    Brand: Sheridan's
    Alcohol type: Coffee liqueurs
    Flavour: Coffee
    Alcohol: 15.5% alc./vol.

Sheridan's is a liqueur first introduced in 1994. It is produced in Dublin by Thomas Sheridan & Sons.

It is uniquely bottled, consisting of two separate sections, separated by glass, but fused. One section is filled with a black liqueur, consisting of coffee and whiskey flavors, while the other is filled with a white liqueur of milk white chocolate with vanilla.

Sheridans Coffee Layered Liqueur.[64]

Caffè Borghetti

Caffè Borghetti, crafted from Ugo Borghetti's original 1860 recipe, is the true espresso coffee liqueur.

It was originally made to celebrate the inauguration of the famous Italian Pescara-Ancona railway line.

Aromatic, with a sweet, soft, enveloping taste, Caffè Borghetti has a rich and intense aroma and a pleasant aftertaste of espresso coffee, capable of conquering on every occasion. The product reflects the Italian traditions that have become the hallmark of our culture.

Alcohol type: Coffee liqueurs

Flavor: Coffee

Alcohol: 25% alc./vol.

Caffè Borghetti.[65]

Patron XO Cafe Tequila

Patrón Xo Cafe is an extraordinary blend of ultra-premium Patrón Silver tequila and the pure, natural essence of fine coffee, sourced from the Mexican states of Veracruz and Chiapas.

The dark, delicious blend of Patron Silver Tequila and the essence of fine coffee results in a dry, not sweet flavor as with most low-proof coffee liqueurs. Excellent for sipping, in cocktails, or as a dessert ingredient.

Alcohol: 35% alc./vol.

Alcohol type: Tequila with coffee

Flavor: Coffee

Alcohol: 35% alc./vol.

Patron XO Cafe Tequila.[66]

Conker Cold Brew Coffee Liqueur

Conker Cold Brew Coffee Liqueur is made in Dorset, combining the distillery's spirit with cold-press coffee from Brazil and Ethiopia. This has notes of vanilla and caramel with real espresso flavor. Delicious on its own over ice, or as a replacement in cocktails for Kahlua and other coffee liqueurs.

Alcohol type: Coffee liqueurs
Flavor: Coffee
Alcohol: 25% alc./vol

Conker Cold Brew Coffee Liqueur.[67]

COFFEE CAN BE ALCOHOLIC COCKTAIL

Irish coffee

According to legend, it was created in 1940 when Joseph Sheridan wanted to warm up a group of passengers who landed at a cold Irish airport.

Served in an Irish Coffee glass.

It is made by pouring 50 ml of Irish whiskey into the glass and adding a teaspoon of sugar or 5 ml of sugar syrup. As for the whiskey, I am a fan of Jameson. The whiskey is heated until it practically boils, i.e., until the sugar dissolves, then continue with extracting espresso up to 120 ml or slightly less over the whiskey and finally top with whipped cream.

Irish coffee.[68]

Espresso Martini

A cocktail that you can recommend after dinner.

Served in a Martini glass.

Fill a shaker with ice, then add 50ml of vodka, 30ml of Kahlua, one shot of espresso, and 10ml of simple syrup. Shake vigorously to create foam inside the shaker. Strain into a chilled glass, and top with the foam that will appear on the top of the drink in the glass with a few coffee beans.

Espresso Martini.[69]

Coffee Corretto

Coffee Corretto is a tradition of Italians.

It is served in a small espresso cup.

An espresso shot is extracted, then a splash of grappa is added to the espresso in the cup, as a rule. Adding grappa is a custom and tradition, although nowadays bartenders often allow guests to choose which alcoholic beverage they want to add. In the past, sambuca was also given as an alternative to grappa, another traditional Italian choice.

I like to serve it by bringing to the guest separately along with the espresso coffee a 20 ml of plum brandy, traditional in our country. This would be the equivalent of grappa in Italy, and then the guests can pour as much as they desire.

Coffee Corretto.[70]

Prairie Buzz

45 ml Rieger's Kansas City whiskey or Scotch Whisky

    15 ml chinato wine

    10 ml amaretto liqueur

    15 ml cold-brew coffee

    15ml heavy cream

    1 bar spoon cinnamon syrup

    Garnish: freshly grated nutmeg

Combine the Kansas City whiskey, or Scotch Whisky, chinato wine, amaretto liqueur, cold-brew coffee, heavy cream, and cinnamon syrup into a shaker and dry shake (without ice). Add ice and shake until well-chilled. Double-strain into a rock glass over a large ice cube. Garnish with freshly grated nutmeg.

This rich, herbaceous, and creamy drink. You can also enjoy it without the addition of coffee if you want a few more glasses.

Prairie Buzz cocktail.[71]

Tequila Espresso Martini

30 ml Blanco tequila

30 ml coffee liqueur

20 ml coffee concentrate or cold brew concentrate

10 ml rich honey syrup (recipe follows)

10 ml Zucca Rabarbaro Amaro

Lemon

Garnish: 3 espresso beans

Add all ingredients to a cocktail shaker filled with 4 ice cubes. Shake vigorously, 15–20 seconds, until chilled. Double-strain through a fine-mesh strainer into a chilled cope glass. Zest a lemon over the cocktail, then discard. Garnish with 3 espresso beans.

To make rich honey syrup: Add 1 cup honey and 1/2 cup water into a small saucepan over medium heat. Stir until the honey is fully dissolved. Allow to cool and transfer to an airtight container. The syrup will keep, refrigerated, for up to 1 month.

Tequila Espresso Martini cocktail.[72]

Oaxacan Tail

30 ml Foro amaro

20 ml mezcal

10 ml Blanco tequila

60 ml cold-brew coffee

15 drops chocolate mole bitters

Add the amaro, mezcal, tequila, coffee, and bitters into a mixing glass with ice and stir until well-chilled.

Strain into an Old Fashioned glass over a large ice cube.

Oaxacan Tail cocktail.[73]

Roman Holiday

30 ml Amaro Meletti

    10 ml Campari

    30 ml cold-brew coffee

    20 ml ounce pineapple juice, freshly squeezed

    20 ml ounce lime juice, freshly squeezed

    10 ml demerara syrup

    1 pinch of sea salt

    Garnish: cinnamon stick

Add the Amaro Meletti, Campari, cold-brew coffee, pineapple juice, lime juice, demerara syrup, and sea salt into a shaker with ice, and shake until well-chilled. Strain into a double rock glass over crushed ice. Garnish with a cinnamon stick.

Roman Holiday cocktail.[74]

Nightcap

60 ml Goslings Gold Seal rum

60 ml cold brew coffee

15 ml grade A maple syrup

Zest of 1 orange

1 dash Angostura bitters

Tonic water, to top

Garnish: orange peel

Add the rum, cold brew, maple syrup, orange zest, and bitters to a shaker with ice and shake until well-chilled. Strain into a highball glass over large ice cubes. Top with the tonic and stir gently. Garnish with an orange peel.

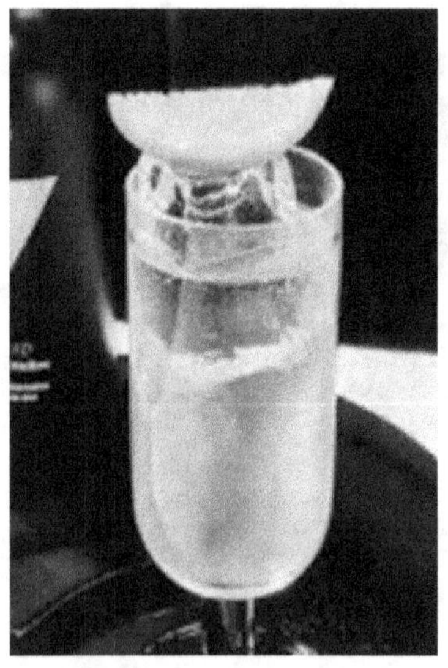

Nightcap cocktail.[75]

Kirsch au Café

30 ml cognac

   20 ml kirsch

   20 ml Cherry Heering

   15 ml simple syrup

   15 ml egg white

   45 ml espresso

Add the cognac, kirsch, Cherry Heering, simple syrup and egg white into a shaker and dry-shake (without ice) vigorously. Add the espresso into the shaker, fill with ice, and shake again until well-chilled. Double-strain into two small cocktail glasses. Coupe glass.

Kirsch au Café cocktail.[76]

Emerald Isle of the Caribbean

45 ml El Dorado Special Reserve 15-year-old rum

15 ml cinnamon syrup

15 ml B.G. Reynolds Don's Spices #2

10 ml velvet falernum

240 ml dark-roast coffee, freshly brewed

Garnish: Tiki whipped cream

Add all ingredients into a large mug and stir to combine. Top with a Tiki whipped cream.

Tiki whipped cream: Add 240 ml heavy cream, 15 ml St. Elizabeth allspice dram, 5 ml Angostura bitters, and 1 tablespoon demerara sugar into a bowl and whip with a stick blender for 30 seconds or until frothy and thickened.

Emerald Isle of the Caribbean cocktail.[77]

WHY WE DRINK COFFEE

People love coffee for various reasons, and the affection for this beverage goes beyond just the aroma and taste. Here are a few key reasons why coffee holds a special place in many people's hearts:

One of the main reasons people love coffee is its caffeine content. Caffeine is a natural stimulant that helps improve focus, alertness, and overall cognitive function. It provides the necessary energy to kickstart the day or get through the mid-afternoon slump.

Coffee has a unique way of bringing people together. Whether meeting a friend for a chat at a café, catching up with colleagues over a cup of coffee, or enjoying a morning drink with family, coffee is often associated with socializing and bonding.

For many, coffee is more than a beverage - it's a ritual. The process of brewing coffee, the aroma filling the room, and the act of sipping a warm cup can be comforting and grounding. It becomes part of daily routines and rituals that provide a sense of familiarity and comfort.

Coffee is incredibly diverse, with a wide range of brewing methods, beans, and flavors to choose from. Whether you prefer a strong espresso, creamy latte, or simple black coffee, there is a coffee style to suit every taste.

Naturally, the taste and aroma of coffee play a significant role in why people love it. The rich, complex flavors of coffee beans, bitterness balanced with sweetness, and enticing aroma wafting from a freshly brewed cup all contribute to its allure.

Represents the overall impression of the density of coffee in the right dosage, with quality foam that we get on the palate and in the mouth, including the mentioned taste and aroma.

Research has shown that moderate coffee consumption can have various health benefits, such as reducing the risk of certain diseases, improving cognitive functions, and speeding up metabolism. Knowing that your favorite beverage can also have positive effects on your health can contribute to your love for coffee.

Coffee has cultural significance in many societies around the world. From traditional coffee ceremonies in Ethiopia to coffee culture in Europe and specialty coffee in the United States, coffee plays a vital role in various cultural practices and traditions.

Personal enjoyment: Ultimately, people love coffee because they enjoy it. Whether it's the first sip of the morning drink, a pleasant cup during a rainy day, or a refreshing cold coffee during the summer heat, as well as the pleasure of trying a new coffee blend, the simple act of drinking coffee brings joy and satisfaction to many.

These are just some of the reasons why people love coffee. The combination of taste, aroma, social connection, rituals, and health benefits contributes to making coffee a favorite beverage for millions around the world. People drink coffee for various reasons, and understanding the essence of this habit can be quite thematic. Here are some common reasons why people enjoy coffee:

Energy Boost: Many seek the energy and focus provided by caffeine, especially to kickstart the day or get through a busy schedule.

Health Benefits: Coffee is linked to numerous health advantages, including disease protection and support for brain and liver health.

Physical Dependence: Some individuals may develop a caffeine addiction, making coffee a regular part of their routine.

Cultural Significance: For many, coffee consumption is deeply rooted in their culture and daily rituals.

Taste: Simply put, many people just love the taste of coffee.

These elements can be woven into a thematic depiction of coffee drinking, emphasizing not only the beverage itself, but also the experiences.

Coffee is one of the most consumed commodities in the world. Travel to any corner of the globe, and you are sure to see someone enjoying coffee in one form or another. Of course, brewing methods may vary, and when people drink coffee depends on their culture and habits. But, one way or another, people everywhere drink coffee.

As much as we would like to say that the number one reason people drink coffee is because they enjoy the taste, it's much more likely that a significant portion of coffee drinkers are chasing the energy boost they get from caffeine. In an increasingly busy world, people need an edge to keep them going as they manage work, raise families, and try to find some time for fun.

A cup of coffee until three in the morning has enough caffeine to give an average-weight person a decent energy boost. Caffeine in coffee blocks adenosine – a neurotransmitter that causes drowsiness and helps people power through their day when they need more sleep. Caffeine can also aid in enhancing focus and improving one's mood, which is desirable for most people.

Coffee also holds many health benefits, mainly due to its caffeine content. Many studies have shown that caffeine has several benefits for brain health, including protection against neurodegenerative diseases such as Parkinson's and Alzheimer's disease, and improvement of long-term memory.

However, the health benefits of coffee are not limited to the brain. Some research shows that regular coffee consumption reduces the risk of liver cirrhosis and supports colon health. There are also some lesser-known benefits of drinking coffee, such as people who drink coffee reporting lower incidence of kidney stones and reduced risk of developing certain cancers, such as prostate cancer, some head and neck cancers, and recurrent breast cancer.

So far, we have only covered the positive reasons why people drink coffee, but there are also some less positive reasons. Caffeine is a psychoactive substance, meaning it can alter brain function. People who regularly consume large amounts of coffee, defined as more than four average-sized cups a day, are at risk of developing caffeine dependence.

Psychological dependence on coffee, although less understood than physical dependence, can prove challenging for individuals who rely on coffee as part of their routine. Paradoxically, these individuals drink coffee just because they drink coffee.

The coffee consumption culture is intertwined with psychological dependence, but it stands out because it transcends everyday routines. For example, the Italian tradition of drinking espresso after dinner is a cultural cornerstone, and for some Italians, skipping coffee would be like going out without clothes, simply unthinkable.

In almost every human culture worldwide, coffee plays a central role in various traditions. Children grow up in families where coffee is enjoyed after meals or as part of holiday customs, and excluding coffee from these experiences seems foreign. Perhaps the most compelling reason is saved for last. Although coffee may be an acquired taste, this doesn't mean that passionate coffee lovers were forced to drink it until they got used to it. Similar to other acquired tastes, once you overcome the initial hurdle, that's when you slowly start to develop a liking for it.

CAFETERIA

A cafeteria is a catering facility and a branch of the hospitality industry. It specializes in light and fast service, primarily serving a wide range of coffee beverages, along with other drinks and light meals. The most common meals offered are pastries and sandwiches. Cafeterias are most popular and busiest in the morning and during the day.

The service is often self-service, although many cafeterias also provide table service with waiters.

Like any other catering facility, it has its own standards and company SOP rules.

Cafeterias follow food safety regulations, especially when it comes to the proper storage and procedures related to coffee, as well as the sensitive ingredient milk, which plays a significant role in preparing various types of coffee and whipped cream.

Safety is also crucial for toppings, cakes, and the food served, which usually arrives already prepared with short shelf lives.

Food usually arrives already prepared with short expiration dates. It must have clear labels for each product separately, so careful attention must be paid when ordering goods, and monitoring sales to track procurement for future orders.

FIFO standards are important to prevent unnecessary waste. FIFO stands for **First In First Out**. The first items received are the first to be sold.

Cafeteria guests expect to be quickly and efficiently served. This is enabled by well-trained, agile, and courteous staff. Products must meet standards to be identical every time a guest orders their favorite coffee or other items from the menu. Any deviation is immediately noticeable and can lead to discontent or loss of customers.

Cafeterias must have the same espresso as a base at all times, with the same taste, aroma, appearance, and volume. This is achieved by professional baristas calibrating the espresso grinder three times a day and recording the results in a dedicated book. Any deviations must be resolved immediately by calibrating the grinder, a task performed by a professional barista. Check the espresso grinder calibration in the section describing the grinder and its calibration.

Professionalism, training, and kindness ensure a safe and positive outcome alongside standards.

Cafeteria staff, like in all hospitality establishments, must maintain personal hygiene and keep the premises clean. This includes tied-back hair, minimal jewelry, subtle makeup, neat nails, and a clean uniform.

Colleagues must be clean-shaven or, if they have a beard or mustache, it must be tidy. Perfumes should be mild and refreshing, not overpowering.

The cafeteria manager will introduce you to the company standards, provide the SOP guidelines, and introduce you to their assistant, shift leaders, and team. Training will be provided, and your progress will be evaluated. Success usually comes through dedication, especially in larger cafeteria chains like "Costa Coffee" and "Starbucks". Each country often has its own smaller cafeteria chains. Franchises typically have trainers dedicated to candidate training.

Uniform

The uniform gives guests a sense of professionalism, while team members feel pride and belonging.

The uniform typically consists of a shirt and pants, or for female colleagues, a skirt that must be below the knees. The shirt should be neatly tucked into the pants. Aprons are part of the uniform in cafeterias, along with a mandatory name badge.

As mentioned, the uniform must be clean and ironed, so you will receive at least two shirts and two pairs of pants. It is appropriate to wear darker shoes and socks, preferably black unless specified otherwise by the uniform itself. Neatness is crucial because you probably wouldn't want to be served by untidy and unkempt staff.

Break

Employees use breaks following the contract and labor law. The break is used for phone calls and for occasional smokers to step outside the guests' view to make calls and smoke a cigarette.

VARIOUS APPLIANCES AND EQUIPMENT FOR THE CAFETERIA

When setting up a cafeteria, having the appropriate devices and equipment is essential to ensure smooth operations and efficient serving of a variety of food. Here are some key devices and equipment commonly found in cafeterias that may be a bit more complex than traditional ones:

A professional coffee machine is necessary for quickly preparing large quantities of coffee, as already shown in the book.

Refrigerators, refrigerated counters, and heated or chilled display cases are essential for storing perishable items, beverages, and ingredients at the proper temperature to maintain food freshness and safety.

Food preparation and processing tables provide a designated workspace for ingredient preparation, dish placement, and food handling.

Various shelves for storing goods or packaging.

A professional oven, whether a convection oven or a combination oven, is crucial for baking and reheating food items.

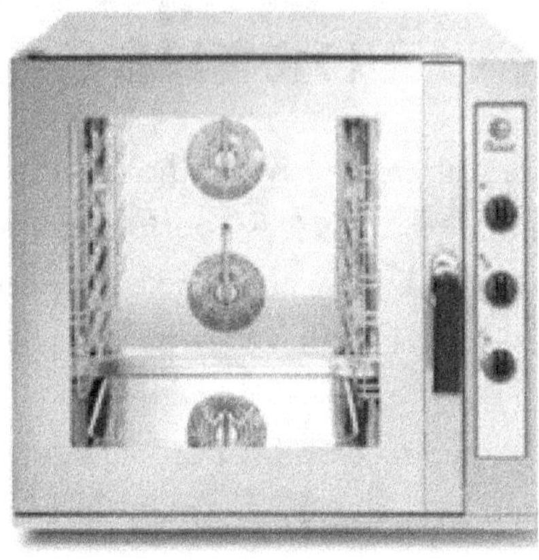

Professional convection oven.[78]

Food warmers help maintain the temperature of hot dishes, soups, and sauces during working hours.

Device for maintaining the heat of food.[79]

Infrared device for maintaining food warmth.[80]

Bain Marie device for maintaining food heat.[81]

A professional dishwasher machine is necessary for efficient cleaning and disinfection of dishes, utensils, and trays used in the cafeteria.

Professional dishwashers.[82]

Food display cases. These cases are used to showcase items that can be picked up and taken away, such as pastries, sandwiches, and other food items that are ready to eat.

Sandwich and other prepared dishes display case. Neatly arranged according to the planogram, clean and well-lit.[83]

Cooling, display case for cakes and pastries.[84]
Hot and cold beverage machines. Blenders and mixers.

Professional blenders and mixers.[85]
Professional ice machine that provides large quantities of ice.

Professional Ice Maker.[86]

Slicers and food processors. These devices are useful for cutting meat and cheese, as well as for food preparation tasks that require chopping or making various purees if part of the food is prepared on-site. There are many different types. It is important to emphasize that we are talking about cafeterias here that deal with a slightly more complex job than traditional cafeterias, yet much simpler than restaurant operations. There is a wide range of tools listed here, and it would be too many pictures if each one was individually shown. It would be a whole catalog, and I hope I have provided the basic guidelines to easily navigate on the internet.

Professional microwave oven: A commercial microwave oven can be handy for quickly heating individual portions or certain foods.

Professional microwave.[87]

The toaster/ Electric panini plate is an indispensable part for heating hot sandwiches.

Double smooth or ribbed plate.[88]

The inventory is of great importance in preparation. Items such as cutting boards, some of which will likely be in prepatration, while others will be on the quick-service counter in the sales area. Bread knives, fruit knives, and other items as needed by the cafeteria. Of course, tongs and similar inventory are also necessary.

Cash register or POS system at the sales point: For processing transactions and efficiently managing sales, a cash register or POS system is essential for processing payments.

These are just a few examples of devices and equipment commonly found in cafeterias. Depending on the menu offerings and the size of the cafeteria, additional specialized equipment may be required. It is important to consider the specific needs of the cafeteria when selecting devices and equipment to help optimize workflow and improve the dining experience for customers while making the job easier for employees.

Significant financial investments are also involved, requiring careful budgeting and reaching set targets to ensure the business is profitable.

This is a long-term business, and it takes time to recoup the investment, but let's not forget that COFFEE HAS THE HIGHEST PROFIT MARGIN in the hospitality industry, although sales volume must be targeted due to the low price of each product sold to customers.

The cafeteria also has an office with video equipment, an IT setup, a safe, and documentation.

Employee locker rooms with restrooms should also be part of such a facility.

COFFEE / LATTE ART

Drawing art on/in coffee, known as latte art or barista art. It is a creative and visually appealing practice that has become synonymous with coffee specialty culture. It involves skillfully pouring steamed/foamed milk into espresso to create a beautiful design on the coffee surface. Coffee art not only enhances the aesthetic appeal of a coffee cup but also showcases the talent and skill of baristas. Baristas worldwide demonstrate their creativity and artistic sense, as well as their ability in their craft.

Creating coffee art requires precision, practice, extensive training, a keen eye for detail, and patience. Baristas carefully steam/froth milk to achieve the correct texture and consistency of milk foam before pouring it into espresso to create various designs. From classic heart patterns, maple leaves, and rosettes to more complex images.

The possibilities for coffee art are endless. Each design reflects the barista's skill and creativity, transforming a simple coffee cup into an artistic masterpiece.

Latte art.[89]

The beauty of coffee art lies in its fleeting nature. The virtual designs created by skilled baristas are temporary, lasting only a few moments before they are stirred and enjoyed by coffee lovers.

The visual pleasure of coffee art adds an element of surprise and excitement to the coffee-drinking experience, making each cup a unique and unforgettable encounter.

Photography plays a key role in preserving and sharing the art of coffee. Photographers eagerly capture the intricate designs, textures, and colors of coffee art, transforming them into stunning images that showcase the beauty and complexity of this craft, the craft of a barista. Through photography, coffee art is immortalized, allowing enthusiasts to appreciate and marvel at these creations long after they have enjoyed them. These works, created by baristas, turn short-lived artistic pieces into eternal art through photography.

Latte art.[90]

The art of coffee has evolved beyond being just a decoration on a coffee cup; it has become a cultural phenomenon that celebrates creativity, craftsmanship, and the joy of coffee culture.

Cafes worldwide showcase the talents of baristas through their unique artistic coffee creations, attracting coffee enthusiasts who appreciate not only the taste but also the art behind their favorite beverage. There are competitions where the best baristas compete, showcasing their passion, skill, and artistry in creating their works.

Coffee art is not just aesthetics; it is a form of expression that combines the art of the barista, the sensory experience of the drinker, and the visual delight of the observer. Whether you enjoy a cozy coffee or appreciate photography, coffee art continues to inspire and captivate coffee lovers worldwide.

NEW TRENDS

120

Coffee tea/ Tea from coffee

Coffee cherry tea is made from the dried husk of the coffee cherry, which is the fruit that surrounds the coffee bean.

Coffee cherry tea, derived from the cherry, has its roots in regions that produce coffee, where the outer fruit of the coffee plant is traditionally discarded as a byproduct of coffee bean processing. However, in recent years, the dried husk or "cascara" has attracted attention as a standalone beverage.

Coffee tea.[91]

Coffee tea/ Tea from coffee typically has a sweet, fruity flavor with hints of hibiscus, cherry, and sometimes a coffee-like undertone. The taste may vary depending on factors such as the coffee variety, processing method, and brewing technique.

To make coffee tea/ tea from coffee, dried coffee cherry husks are steeped in hot water similar to traditional tea. The brewing process can be adjusted to achieve different flavor profiles and strengths.

The art of cold brew coffee

Cold brew coffee is made by steeping coarsely ground roasted and cold coffee beans in cold water for an extended period, typically 12-24 hours. This slow extraction process results in a smooth, rich coffee concentrate.

The choice of coffee beans plays a crucial role in the flavor profile of the cold beverage. Coarsely ground coffee beans are ideal for cold brewing to prevent over-extraction and bitterness. Coarse grinding allows for a slower extraction process and smoother preparation.

Since cold brew coffee is prepared with cold water, using high-quality filtered water is essential to enhance the overall coffee flavor. The steeping time for cold brew can vary depending on personal preferences. Experiment with different brewing times to find the ideal balance between strength and flavor.

After the steeping process is complete, the coffee grounds should be filtered to separate the coffee concentrate. This can be done using a fine mesh sieve, cheesecloth, or a dedicated coffee preparation device.

Cold brew coffee is typically served over ice and can be enjoyed black or with the addition of milk, cream, or sweeteners to taste. It can be stored in the refrigerator for several days, allowing for a refreshing cup of coffee whenever desired.

By mastering the art of cold coffee preparation, you can create a delicious and refreshing beverage with a unique flavor profile that is perfect for hot summer days or as a smooth alternative to hot coffee. Experimenting with different preparation techniques and types of whole-bean coffee can further enhance your cold brew experience.

Coffee cherry tea contains caffeine, but the levels are generally lower than those found in brewed coffee. This makes it a popular choice for those seeking a milder caffeine intake.

Fans of coffee cherry tea claim it contains antioxidants and other beneficial compounds, though more research is needed to fully understand its potential health benefits.

In some regions where coffee is grown, coffee cherry tea has been a traditional beverage for centuries, deeply rooted in local customs and practices.

Cold brew coffee.[92]

Cold brew coffee with milk.[93]

TAKE AWAY

At the beginning of the book, I mentioned that you will often encounter people rushing to work and grabbing coffee on the go. For all of this to be logical and possible, cafes have TAKE AWAY packaging.

Take Away packaging is made from various materials and they must meet certain standards which we will discuss a bit later.

Cups for hot drinks to go.[94]

Cardboard/paper cups are used for hot coffee and drinks to go. The body of the cup is designed in a way that you don't burn yourself while carrying and drinking your coffee. Sometimes they also have paper sleeves around the cup for added safety.

Take Away a cup with a lid, a paper sleeve wrapped around the cup, and a handle.[95]

To prevent coffee from spilling while walking, driving, or similar, there are plastic lids that securely seal the cup with the beverage.

Sometimes it's necessary to carry multiple cups at the same time, perhaps when you're bringing coffee to someone else. For this purpose, cardboard/paper cup carriers for multiple cups simultaneously have been designed. They are usually made for two and four cups.

Plastic cups for cold coffees and drinks to go.[96]

Cups for cold coffee and other beverages are different because they are made of plastic. Typically, these are transparent cups with a plastic lid that can come in various shapes, from flat to domed, suitable for drinks with whipped cream, foam, and similar toppings.

Remaining Take Away packaging.[97]

We have noticed that cafes usually offer light meals and desserts. Light meals typically include various sandwiches and pastries. Our guests often want to take something with them, so every cafe should be equipped with take-out packaging for such products, as well as bags in which multiple items could be packed. This take-out packaging and bags come in various sizes to accommodate different order sizes.

Cardboard/paper eco-friendly straws.[98]

Lately, biodegradable cardboard/paper straws are being increasingly used, especially for takeaway beverages.

Knowing that plastic straws are not biodegradable, it is logical to understand how much cleaner and healthier environment we get by using biodegradable straws. The amount of waste is significantly reduced.

Standards that packaging for take-out must meet

During the last few years, the number of food delivery services has significantly increased. To succeed in the industry, catering establishments must ensure that products are delivered safely, which includes food packaging.

Essentially, food packaging refers to materials that come into direct contact with food. It is crucial to consider the "type of food" and the requirements for the packaging to be certified.

The food industry has strict regulations on the type of packaging that can and cannot come into contact with food. Since food and beverages are consumed, any harmful toxins or unsafe contaminants from the packaging can have catastrophic consequences for consumers.

The primary criterion for food packaging is that it must be non-toxic and safe to come into contact with products that will be consumed. Some examples include takeout coffee cups, sandwich boxes, various containers for takeaway, and any other packaging that can be used for food and beverages.

Therefore, materials for food packaging must be rigorously tested. Additionally, manufacturers must educate their customers on how to properly use the packaging. For example, if the packaging material "fails," meaning it becomes harmful at high temperatures and contaminates the contents inside, it is not suitable for hot food and drinks.

The Food and Drug Administration (FDA)

The Food and Drug Administration (FDA) in the US determines food packaging based on a set of criteria. The association offers several educational resources dedicated to its expectations for food materials, prohibited substances, and other relevant information that packaging manufacturers and owners of food and catering companies must adhere to.

The FDA website not only addresses food safety expectations but also the impact on the environment and all other concerns and regulations related to food packaging.

There are many ways in which businesses can identify how to obtain reliable, certified food packaging. For example, an HACCP (Hazard Analysis & Critical Control Point) plan will outline the risks associated with food packaging suppliers.

Being able to identify where food contact will occur, and the materials involved is the responsibility of the company owner and management team. Non-compliance with food safety standards can lead to health risks for consumers.

Additionally, it can result in negative customer experiences and cost the business money and products.

It is important to look for several certifications when sourcing products for food packaging.

These are some of the certifications from the National Sanitation Foundation (NSF) that you can expect to see on food packaging labels.

BRCGS Certificate

BRCGS (Brand Reputation through Compliance Global Standard) certificate is a globally recognized certification that covers not only food packaging production but also food and ingredient production, as well as gluten-free production and storage logistics.

This certificate demonstrates that the packaging is made in accordance with food safety standards and meets globally recognized criteria.

IFS Certificate

Another global certification, the International Featured Standard (IFS) certification focuses on both food and consumer product packaging. The criteria standards relate to product sourcing, packaging production, manufacturing processes, and safe food storage.

This is a valuable certificate that provides an additional layer of security to ensure the validity of food packaging claims.

NSF and FDA

The National Sanitation Foundation (NSF) offers these certificates and more based on the packaging you create for food. NSF ensures FDA compliance, making their certificates well-known and respected throughout the industry.

While these certificates are vital for demonstrating safety, the FDA certificate and logo indicating "food type" status are the ultimate certifications to look for on packaging.

There are several NSF certifications to consider, but just know that FDA compliance is required to meet food standards. Alternatively, NSF compliance shows that you are going above and beyond to meet safe guidelines for your food products, processes, and packaging.

FDA (Food and Drug Administration) food logo

The international food logo is an image of a glass and fork placed side by side. If this logo is present on any packaging, it indicates it can safely come into contact with food.

Moreover, you still need to adhere to all protocols and functions specified by the packaging manufacturer to prevent materials from becoming harmful. However, this logo guarantees that the packaging can be used and can come into contact with food products without worrying about contamination.

Another regulatory body that will set standards for food packaging is the Environmental Protection Agency (EPA). EPA will help ensure that waste associated with packaging does not harm the environment.

CHECKLIST

The checklist represents the format of points formatted as questions for checking the status of standards in the cafeteria prescribed by the company's SOP. They often include a part of the check related to rules/ definitions and laws prescribed by the state law.

The mentioned cafeteria check form known as the Checklist is not something to be misunderstood and considered solely as criticism that follows. Adhering to standards reduces the percentage of negatives you will earn in the checklist review, and where there are errors in the cafeteria, the checklist will show what needs to be worked on, what needs to be checked, even dedicated training, mostly what needs to be corrected to bring your cafeteria back on track with the company's SOP.

It is important to work on error corrections based on suggestions after the check. So, it is still a suggestion, not criticism. What is not good is if the same mistake is repeated or it is evident that no work has been done on correcting the error based on suggestions. That is then a problem that can lead to certain sanctions according to the employment contract.

Checklist is usually conducted by the company's internal control, and the cafeteria manager should have the same Checklist and perform checks on their cafeteria and colleagues. This routine conducted by the manager brings the cafeteria to a high level, familiarizes colleagues with the importance of meeting prescribed standards, and trains them while reducing their anxiety from internal control, which can often create psychological issues for employees, especially young and inexperienced ones, leading to mistakes due to anxiety and misunderstanding of the cafeteria's condition check.

Franchises are obligated to have such a document in their procedures, and I recommend that even the owner of a single cafeteria follows the same principle. Going through the list will always remind you to be thorough and not overlook details in checks.

What should this document contain, and what have I seen, done, and participated in regarding Checklists?

This document contains main headings and questions under each title, such as:

- Quality of beverages

In this heading, there will be questions like: Is the coffee dosage standard and how many grams is it? I have encountered different standards, for example, where the standard dose for an espresso is 7g of ground coffee and in other cafeterias where the standard is between 8 and 8.2g of ground coffee.

Does 30ml expire during extraction for 20 seconds?

Are calibration documents for coffee filled out?

Quality of milk foam, is it made according to regulations?

Is the milk temperature monitored, etc.? It may also contain questions about pressure in the espresso machine.

- Hygiene

In this section, attention will be paid to the approach to the cafeteria and entrance to the cafeteria. Just as the inspector enters, the list of questions should guide them to check the cleanliness of the café garden, hygiene, and arrangement of tables and chairs. Further checks include whether external advertisements are working, and all lights are on, and then move to the inside of the cafeteria checking the cleanliness of entrance doors, and the smell inside the cafeteria.

Then cleanliness and arrangement of tables, observing the lower parts of the table such as legs or bases, of course, cleanliness of floors, light fixtures, lamps, bulbs, and if they are all functioning properly.

Check the cleanliness of the walls and if the ventilation is working properly, as well as air conditioning units.

After this part, the cleanliness and equipment of the toilet are checked.

- Other drinks and food

This section involves checking the dates, labels, and FIFO standards.

Then, ensuring that everything is served according to standards.

Equipment and small inventory are also checked because chipped glasses or cups should not be in use. It is important to document and sign the waste list daily. These are presented in multiple questions and items, I am listing just a portion to give an idea of what is being done.

- Team

This involves the team members themselves. For example, the prescribed service speed, smile, and courtesy, cleanliness of uniforms, and personal hygiene.

Items often include questions related to the sales procedure and whether it is done according to standards and training.

Attention is also given to whether employees respect break times and related regulations.

- Marketing program

Involves checking the menu, brochures, flyers, business cards, acrylic displays, and A-frames. Attention is also given to ensuring there are no flyers or similar content from other companies.

- Rules by the Law

This section focuses on compliance with the laws and regulations prescribed by the state in which the cafeteria operates. For example, regulations regarding working hours and whether they are displayed as required. Legal notices that must be displayed and similar. Cafeteria chains may have their cafeterias in destinations where not all regulations are uniformly prescribed by law, and differences must be respected and properly monitored.

This is a part of the job usually handled by regional and operational managers who guide the cafeteria manager in complying. They provide him with the necessary tools so that he and his colleagues can adhere to these regulations.

OBSERVATION OF THE COMPETITION

Having information about the competition and cafeterias in the area is crucial for success. By understanding the offerings, prices, preferences/ desires, and needs of competitor's guests, a cafeteria can identify its unique selling points and areas for improvement. This knowledge helps in creating a strategic marketing plan, setting competitive prices, and developing unique coffee and beverage menus, and menus that cater to the local community. Ultimately, being informed about the competition and cafeterias in the area enables a cafeteria to remain relevant, attract more customers, and thrive in a competitive market.

Monitoring the competition and cafeterias in the neighborhood allows your cafeteria to adapt to changing trends and guest preferences. It also provides valuable insights into potential partnerships or collaborations from which both businesses can benefit.

By staying informed and proactive in keeping up with the local coffee scene, a cafeteria can position itself as a destination for coffee lovers and establish a strong presence in the community.

Sometimes, small details are needed to achieve great success.

SALES AND INCREASE IN SALES

Sales and increasing sales, why is it so important?

Material, small inventory, equipment, and a range of elements are needed to create a product that, along with quality service, embodies the hospitality act. This is how I would briefly describe it. Based on the above, we can get a certain idea of the level of challenge in achieving and exceeding the set target that is budgeted, when we look at the mentioned items from the perspective of what is needed to achieve them. For example, how much various small inventory we must have and maintain, not to mention the process of providing proper service – these are just two examples I used to explain from the definition I provided.

All this prompts us, guides us back, and warns us that traditional sales based on phrases like "Is that all?" or "Would you like anything else?" do not help increase sales, which is crucial for all the reasons mentioned above. As you have probably noticed, I often write about increasing sales and emphasize its importance because it is of great significance in achieving results. I have made an effort and continue to do so to make my colleagues salespersons, to guide the guest towards their suggestions and sell what will delight the guest and lead them to spend more than they had planned, rather than just letting them dictate what they have read from the menu, drink list, ... And most importantly: to be satisfied and not regret spending a little more.

Just think, would you rather have a Latte or a Vanilla Latte for a minimal extra charge? Now multiply that, the minimal extra charge for the vanilla flavor, by the daily number, monthly, and ultimately yearly, where we will reach a nice "figure," and I have taken the simplest example. Many such ideas will come to your mind over time if you dedicate yourself to it with sincere enthusiasm. These are the real points for budgeting, exceeding targets, and the basis for earning rewards on your earnings. By offering nice suggestions, you have satisfied the guest's taste and already secured a gratuity, a returning guest.

For a quality increase in sales and profit, experts in sales in the field they specialize in are needed. Every earned "point" in any currency above expectations is obtained through SUGGESTIVE SELLING. Let's take coffee as an example where it is advisable to go with a medium offer. The goal is not to go for cheaper options and thereby please the guests or cheer them up with a low bill. When you are confident in the positive reaction of the guest, boast that you also have a better option available, if you notice interest. At that point, you completely leave the choice to the guest and suggest quality. I recommend showing on the menu what you offer so that the guest is informed about the price, to avoid them feeling deceived later on.

Of course, everything has its limits, and years of experience are needed for professional sales.

MARKETING

In a dynamic marketing environment, hospitality businesses constantly seek innovative ways to reach guests. While modern social media platforms have revolutionized how brands connect with consumers in various industries, traditional marketing tools such as A-boards, flyers, and business cards still play a vital role in a comprehensive marketing strategy. By integrating traditional and digital channels, hospitality businesses can create a cohesive and impactful marketing campaign that maximizes brand visibility, drives engagement, and delivers tangible results.

The Importance of A-Frames and Clear Signage

A-frames, also known as sidewalk signs, are a classic yet effective way to attract passersby and promote businesses. Strategically placed outside storefronts or building entrances, A-frames are attractive displays that convey key messages and promotions to pedestrians. They capture the attention of passersby securely. Clear signage, whether on windows, doors, or walls, strengthens the brand identity and helps pedestrians or visitors easily locate and identify the hospitality establishment. In an increasingly competitive market, having clear and visually appealing signs is essential to stand out and attract the attention of potential guests.

The Power of Flyers and Business Cards

Flyers and business cards are tangible marketing materials that leave a lasting impression on customers. Flyers are versatile tools for promoting events, sales, or new products, while business cards serve as a professional representation of the brand and its representatives. Despite the digital age, the nature of flyers and business cards adds a personal touch to marketing efforts and helps establish a physical connection with customers. Sharing well-designed flyers or business cards can leave an unforgettable impact and encourage further engagement with the brand.

Utilizing the Reach of Modern Social Media

In today's digital era, social media has become indispensable platforms for connecting businesses with their target audience. Platforms such as Facebook, Instagram, Twitter, and LinkedIn offer unparalleled reach and targeting capabilities, enabling brands to engage with customers in real time and tailor their messages to specific demographic categories. Social media marketing allows businesses to build brand awareness, drive traffic to their website, and foster customer loyalty through content engagement, partnerships with influencers, and targeted advertising campaigns.

Synergy of Traditional and Digital Marketing Channels

While modern social media platforms provide broad reach and instant connectivity, traditional marketing tools offer tangible and personal touches that complement digital efforts. By integrating old-school methods like A-frames, clear signage, flyers, and business cards with modern social media strategies, businesses can create a cohesive and multi-faceted marketing approach that maximizes brand visibility and customer engagement. It distinctly highlights the personal touch of a hospitality establishment. The synergy between traditional and digital channels enables companies to leverage the advantages of each platform and create a memorable and impactful brand presence at various touchpoints.

The importance of A-frames, clear signage, flyers, business cards, and modern social media in a comprehensive marketing strategy cannot be overstated. By combining the best of traditional and digital marketing channels, companies can create an approach that resonates with customers, promotes brand awareness, and ultimately leads to business success.

Website

A website serves as a crucial marketing tool for businesses.

Website is often the first interaction potential customers have with your brand/ company. A well-designed site can leave a positive impression and encourage further engagement.

Websites constantly collect valuable data about user behavior, preferences, and demographics. This information helps you refine your marketing strategies.

A strong website establishes your legitimacy and credibility. It's a place where customers can learn about your offerings, read testimonials, and trust your brand.

The website allows you to showcase your products and services effectively, providing detailed information and visuals to potential customers.

A well-optimized website improves your search engine rankings, making it easier for people to find you online.

Websites offer a platform to share valuable content (such as blog posts, videos, or guides) that educates and engages your audience

FOOD AND BEVERAGE SAFETY

I assume that all restaurateurs, as well as collaborators in the procurement of food and beverages for hospitality establishments, are owners of a valid health/ sanitary card. It serves as the basis for starting work in a hospitality establishment and represents a confirmation of satisfactory biological, physical, and even mental examination.

It happens that due to a minor injury on the finger, growth, or the presence of bacteria in the nose (for example, due to a recent cold), a candidate does not receive a passing grade and a certified health/ sanitary card for work. There is no need to worry excessively; instead, with an explanation, visit your doctor, and start the recommended therapy. Make an effort to heal through sick leave until the rescheduled health/ sanitary examination. Never return to work if the health/ sanitary inspection has not been satisfactory, as you may cause problems for the company and yourself in case of inspection by the competent state authorities. Moreover, it is ethically correct to heal before resuming work.

It is necessary to be familiar with the topic of food and beverage storage: storage temperature, whether it is possible to keep a certain food frozen or not, as well as the expiration date. It is important to know which foods must be stored in special boxes, bags, etc., as well as how foods are allowed to be grouped in the refrigerator or freezer. It would not be nice if, for example, a fruit gets the smell of another food. For this reason, there are storage plans to follow. They are usually pasted on the doors of refrigerators, freezers, cold rooms, or chambers. The most important thing is to avoid cross-contamination of food, and the creation, and spread of various infections.

Employee hygiene and their approach to food are crucial factors in avoiding cross-contamination: proper hand washing and disinfection, clean and appropriate use of uniforms for specific tasks, and gloves. Using different utensils for different products and different utensils for different temperature states, from frozen to hot. Utensils used for hot products should not be used on products in the cold section. Likewise, utensils used for fruit should not be used for meat or similar products as they can cause cross-contamination and compromise health.

Declarations are documents that must accompany all "goods" as they guarantee the accuracy, content, recipe (e.g., cake), production date, freezing date, and expiration date. Shelf life after thawing. It is important to know how long and at what temperature foods can be stored. Declarations can take various forms, even as small stickers. Even bottles of beverages have them.

Hospitality business, like other industries, has prescribed rules on how various surfaces are washed, cleaned, and disinfected. There are procedures for daily hygiene maintenance, as well as weekly and monthly schedules. It is important to know exactly which chemical agents are used to guarantee health safety and disinfection. The dedication to hygiene can be easily seen in the area where stewards work. Usually, their walls are covered with all instructions and cleaning, washing, and disinfection supplies.

When receiving food and beverage supplies, it is necessary to consult with the supplier about storage methods and temperatures. The receiving record, waybill, invoice, or receipt of the goods that arrived must have the seal and signature of the supplier, the signature of the deliverer, and the recipient. The recipient's signature confirms that the received goods have been inspected by the responsible person in the company for receiving goods. This person cannot be just anyone in the company but must be a professionally trained individuals.

DDD - Disinfection, Desinsection, and Deratization are essential practices that must also meet the requirements for operating in a hospitality establishment. Authorized companies are responsible for these tasks and provide a service expiration date after their intervention. It is necessary to repeat the process before the expiration date to prevent rodent, insect, or similar issues. If a problem arises before the deadline, the DDD company must be called immediately to honor their guarantee. These interventions are carried out outside the establishment's operating hours. If any staff member notices insects or rodents, they should report them to their superiors promptly, as these pests can transmit diseases and pose a danger to guests and employees. It is also unpleasant for guests to encounter such situations. Reports should be made discreetly, of course.

WHAT IS HACCP?

The term you will often hear mentioned in catering establishments or come across a sign with this designation. Lately, in butcher shops and stores, you will find the HACCP mark on a certain number of products. This is an abbreviation of **Hazard Analysis Critical Control Point**. It is a certification confirming that a specific catering establishment meets the conditions for receiving, storing, and handling goods, from the warehouse, through the preparation area, process and production area, and work processes to further aspects of food and beverages, including service, all aimed at preventive action against contamination of raw materials, disease transmission, and anything hazardous to health.

The process and production part in cafeterias is the space that in a restaurant would be the kitchen, but the restaurant kitchen is much more complex, which is why in a cafeteria it is called the process and production part.

HACCP also ensures proper storage methods to prevent the mixing of odors, contact between different food items, separation of thermally processed from raw foods, and everything needed to avoid cross-contamination. It even dictates which cleaning, disinfecting, etc. agents can be used and how.

You will often come across posted diagrams on the wall showing how items are arranged in a refrigerated display case, refrigerator, cold room, chamber, warehouse, and the like.

When implementing HACCP, you will notice that wooden boards are no longer used, nor are wooden blocks for cutting and chopping large pieces. Wooden spoons are also eliminated, along with anything that could be a possible source of cross-contamination. Silicone and temperature-resistant plastic spoons are used instead. HACCP has its own rules for straws accompanying beverages.

StockChiller

Standard Operating Procedures
with Hazard Analysis Critical Control Point Plan

CCP 1

- Check that your prepared food is above the critical temperature: 190°F
  Method: Temperature Sensor | Potential Hazards: Biological

CCP 2

- Examine that the storage containers are clean and sanitary. Check the container gasket.
  Method: Visual inspection | Potential Hazards: Biological, Physical, Chemical

CCP 3

- Transfer food into containers preventing cross contamination. Record temperature, time, seal lid. Chill in Countertop Stock Chiller Unit using sufficient ice: 8 lbs of ice for every 1 gallon of soup.
  Method: Visual, Temperature Sensor, and Timer | Potential Hazards: Biological, Physical

CCP 4

- Turn off unit once ice has completely melted. On the initial cycle, open the container and account for the gasket in or out of the lid. Record temperature, time, date, and batch number. Verify the temperature is not above critical temperature of 35°F.
  Method: Visual, Temperature Sensor, and Clock | Potential Hazards: Biological, Physical

CCP 5

- Initial Test Batches: Reseal container if temperature in CCP 4 is satisfactory. Adjust ice quantity as needed.
  Method: Data log | Potential Hazards: Biological
- All other Cycles: Do not open containers if the same amount of ice is used to chill as the initial cycle. Update label on the container.
  Method: Data log | Potential Hazards: Biological

CCP 6

- Move product into cold storage using first in first out rotation. Make sure cold storage temperature is not higher than the critical limit: 38°F
  Method: Visual inspection | Temperature Sensor | Potential Hazards: Biological

Fridge organization chart

Arrange shelves by cooking temperature - highest cooking temperature on the bottom.

Ready-to-Eat Foods (top shelf)

Lowest cooking temperature

57°C

Any food that will be hot held that is not in other categories

63°C

Whole seafood; beef, pork, veal, lamb (steaks and chops); roasts; eggs that will be served immediately

68°C

Ground, injected, marinated, or tenderized meats; eggs that will be hot held

74°C

All poultry (chicken, turkey, duck, fowl); stuffing made with foods that require temperature control; dishes with previously cooked foods (casseroles)

Highest cooking temperature

WASTE

Waste is a word commonly heard in conversations among managers. In discussions between a Director and a Manager. What constitutes waste? It's everything that is unnecessary and sometimes carelessly discarded.

Carelessly and excessively use, what we write off/discard due to expiration dates, errors, and the like. Justified waste is only training waste and the first spilled coffees after cleaning the machine or espresso machine handles. Each cafeteria has a certain percentage of approved waste. It is approved through budget projections. Anything beyond that is unacceptable. In practice, you'll probably catch yourself crumpling and throwing away paper napkins without thinking, or pouring out an unnecessarily measured amount of milk even though, by standards, it's usable. The usual mindset for these issues is: 'Oh, there's plenty of this.' 'This small thing won't matter to the company'... Often, individuals are unaffected by such matters and find it easier to throw away a lot rather than neatly store it, even though by standard it is suitable for further use.

Ignorance is often the problem. However, it is important to adhere to the standards and not break them by excessive attempts to save. When unnecessary discarded napkins, quantities of toothpicks, stirrers, purées, coasters, truffles, sponges are added up on a weekly, monthly, and yearly basis, a significant amount is reached. Here, only some items from the cafeteria are mentioned, resulting in a sum that could cover several salaries.

Waste is also caused by carelessness. Careless coordination of expiration dates of various individual items or materials for preparation.

Unprofessional use of inventory is also a problem that causes high costs, such as breaking small inventory, damaging various equipment, and so on.

Without delving deeper into this topic, I want to emphasize the importance of responsibility in preserving the company as the hand that feeds you.

How waste is created. In short, examples include: pouring milk incorrectly for steaming or spilling some of the foam to reach the desired instead of properly steaming the milk.

Insufficiently or improperly tamped coffee in the handle of an espresso machine will result in bad coffee that cannot be served to a guest. If it is weakly or unevenly tamped in the handle, it will leak too quickly and you will get weak coffee with poor foam. Over-tamped coffee produces burnt, slow-flowing coffee with black foam. So, you cannot serve that to a guest either, and there goes the waste.

One of the reasons is improper storage according to the FIFO standard, resulting in receiving products with expired shelf life instead of being issued based on the First In First Out principle.

There are many more examples, but from these, you can see the extent of damage caused by negligence that can be prevented with a little effort.

How to avoid waste? It is avoided through education, training, attention, dedication, timeliness, and data recording. Also, through analyses that you can create yourself, even easier with the help of supervisors and data from the system.

The impact on the budget based on waste? The more waste, the less room for profit, and therefore less leverage for seeking higher pay or bonuses. This is meant for the well-being of the household so that the household can think of you. Basic knowledge of small inventory and consumables is essential. The easiest way to learn about small inventory is by visiting the websites of reputable companies that supply it. These companies usually offer the option to download a catalog in PDF format, providing a great solution for expanding hospitality knowledge. Through small inventory and equipment, you can learn a lot about the hospitality industry.

From the very beginning of the book, I present a specific topic along with examples of small inventory and equipment, providing the groundwork and guidance for further learning on the said topic.

Frequent breakage, for example, demonstrates negligence towards small inventory. Small inventory for professional hospitality is quite expensive. It also impacts the results of the targeted budget.

During waste disposal after service, it sometimes happens that something from the small inventory is accidentally discarded in the trash due to haste. It's usually spoons, forks, knives, or other utensils, and even other inventory. This is one of the reasons for increasing waste, which is undesirable.

CAFETERIA TERRACE

Like at other hospitality venues, the terrace is always popular with the first rays of sun after a cold and rainy winter. All café terraces and other hospitality venues can be seen operating at full capacity. People breathe in fresh air, enjoy the warm days, and keep the hosts busy.

Serving the garden is physically more challenging due to the distance from the main units. However, this can be organized with the help of auxiliary staff who get engaged. Satisfaction should reign throughout the collective because as soon as there is work, everyone benefits with better earnings.

During the summer, it's logical for people to use the terraces since a few will opt for the indoor space with air conditioning, especially now that there are specific refreshers for terraces. In autumn, everyone knows winter is approaching, so they often use the last warm days to sit outside. However, a terrace is not a space that is easily maintained, cleaned, secured, protected, etc. Besides the good earnings, it requires care and dedication.

Variable weather conditions often trouble restaurateurs with setting up and taking down their outdoor terraces. Colleagues often look for excuses not to redo everything if rain or wind, for example, returns. One should not be lazy in such situations; if you see a change, redefine the setup, as that is part of our job. Unless you are sure that the bad weather will be short-lived. In spring and autumn, you may find yourself setting up and taking down the terrace 5-6 times a day.

The biggest issue is keeping sponge cushions and leather menus dry to prevent damage.

Wind is also a major threat to open terraces, as it can cause significant material damage and injuries. Therefore, it's essential to monitor the weather forecast daily, consult with superiors, suggest improvements, and report anything unusual. Failing to recognize the wind's cues can turn an unprepared staff and location into a disastrous outcome. You can find evidence of such results online, with an example below the next lines of text.

Let's imagine a situation where, for example, the staff did not react quickly enough, and a large umbrella on the terrace is swept away by a strong gust of wind as light as a feather, ending up on a nearby car, causing damage due to the force of the wind and its weight. This can have serious consequences for passersby, guests at the establishment where you work, or in the vicinity. At first, it may seem trivial and not problematic, with common phrases like "We'll do it later," "We have time," and "Maybe nothing will happen," but when the consequences arise, it will be too late. Therefore, laziness should not be justified.

A-frames and similar outdoor advertisements should not be placed in similar situations as well. Anything not properly secured poses a threat. I know I haven't written anything new in these lines, but I emphasize that I write from my experience or what I have seen to help new colleagues and remind experienced ones.

Colleagues often bring habits from their previous workplace when transitioning to a new one and may not immediately notice what needs attention. For this reason, it is recommended that whenever entering a new facility, look for what was previously mentioned: SOPs, and consult with superiors and colleagues about everything.

During windy days, it is often necessary to stack chairs in one group and secure them, and often tables as well, depending on the material and weight.

Disaster on the terrace was caused by negligence and neglect of the threat of severe weather.[99]

RELATIONSHIP WITH GUESTS AND COLLEAGUES

In the cafeteria, the relationship between guests and cafeteria staff is valued. The goal is to create a warm and pleasant atmosphere where mutual respect, excellent service, and friendly interactions thrive. The team is dedicated to ensuring that every guest feels welcome and appreciated.

The relationship between cafeteria staff and guests is an important aspect of the experience in this hospitality establishment. This includes mutual respect, communication, and understanding. The staff should provide friendly and efficient service to guests with a positive attitude.

Clear communication between staff and guests is essential. This includes listening to feedback, answering questions, and providing information about the menu and the preparation of drinks and food. Genuine suggestions are what guests appreciate.

Guests expect a high standard of service, including cleanliness, promptness, and accuracy in orders. The staff should strive to meet these expectations.

The staff should be open to guest feedback, using it to improve their service and overall experience in the restaurant. Similarly, guests should acknowledge and appreciate the efforts of the staff.

Veteran hospitality professionals often become skilled psychologists. I would recommend to any young colleague entering our field to attend at least one seminar or basic NLP course. NLP, or Neuro-Linguistic Programming, is an education that helps in understanding the psyche of the interlocutor and provides a good direction in the science of sales. This is how I experienced it and how I would prefer to describe and define this science in the context of hospitality. This is the shortest definition I can give based on my experience and attending NLP programming courses. I recommend it not only to the youth as mentioned, but to every professional who comes into direct contact with customers, clients, and guests.

Therefore, it's about Neuro-Linguistic Programming. Perhaps through the very name, you can get a slight idea of what it's about. In these courses, instructors present an incredible number of perspectives on the world around them and emphasize sales if you are inclined towards that part of the course.

By attending the mentioned course, you will learn to observe people, their gestures, facial expressions, body language, tone of voice, and everything else you notice in your interlocutor, to know how to proceed and guide the conversation in your favor, in a positive direction. This can help you gather a lot more information based on a single gesture, movement, expression, hand position, speaking speed, tone of voice, intonation, foot tapping, finger fiddling while the interlocutor speaks to you, how a person looks away when recalling something, and how they look if pretending to recall, essentially fabricating.

It may seem like delving deep into psychology, but I am trying to explain the importance of psychology in our industry, as NLP will be highly beneficial in a crucial topic, the INCREASE IN SALES and suggestive selling.

The first thing to learn is that it is vital that at work and in business, emotions do not exist, only order, hard work, discipline, and professionalism. The sooner we rid ourselves of emotions that affect our work and think in the right direction, the sooner we will be on the path to considering ourselves professionals.

Communicate with colleagues and engage in clear and transparent debates about work without emotional viewpoints. Work on clear and healthy communication with an exchange of ideas and finding the right solution. Involve more knowledgeable or superior colleagues openly and honestly in business debates if necessary, to reach the correct solution.

In our business, ethical norms are important and should be respected and considered as principles of a healthy relationship with any colleague, guest, or company.

A true host will constantly self-assess and strive to perform each action/task/service better than before. Initially, this may feel burdensome, but eventually, it becomes ingrained. Mechanically doing so, remembering actions, and noticing errors, both in others and oneself, to help colleagues or students avoid them.

We learn from others' mistakes to reduce our own, and we try to correct our own. Never by naming who and when made a mistake, but simply as an example of what not to do, then how to do it right during group training sessions. Another approach is offering direct and immediate help to a colleague, for example: "Colleague, I believe you intended to do your best in your opinion, but you need to...". This is how hosts are made, a process passed down through generations. I believe this is the right path to collegiality and healthy team success.

Accept your mistakes, or at least seek advice from a suitable professional if someone points out your errors. Avoid getting angry, being arrogant, or involving feelings of inferiority - it's all part of the job and excludes personal life and factors.

Hospitality, from any point of view, clearly represents a service, but service does not represent hospitality. Service is directed towards the guest. It involves transferring, for example, a product from point A to point B. From the bar or kitchen to the guest, but is that enough!? Hospitality precisely here makes a difference from basic and simple service. The word "hospitality" itself, gives us the word "host," which implies that we will invest additional effort to host someone, show hospitality, joy in being able to provide service in a quality manner, professional, enriched with experience, love for the job, and a smile, while making the hosted person feel comfortable. The guest who pays for hospitality services should not feel like someone who has wasted money but rather received a certain experience greater than just a service from point A to point B.

HEALTH AND SAFETY ABOVE ALL

The topic is not pleasant to write about, but given that we directly address a large part of the topics related to our profession, it is worth considering health and safety at work. I believe that a few tips acquired through years of experience will help, so you don't have to learn things the hard way through your own experience. It will assist in healthier work and prevent some troubles that can significantly hinder your job and quality of life. It directly affects the quality and comfort of life to the extent that we constantly need to analyze our physical and even more so, mental capabilities.

In all sectors, it is important to know fire extinguishing. Different materials, substances, etc. are extinguished in different ways. In the kitchen, for example, you will find a box with a fire blanket on the wall. This mentioned blanket is the best solution for extinguishing a fire in a fryer, but do not lift it until you are sure the fire has been extinguished because if you accidentally lift it at the wrong time, that is, too early, the fire will receive a sudden supply of oxygen and can lead to serious injuries and an even bigger fire.

You must know where the cabinets with emergency supplies are located. Emergency supply cabinets are often neglected. People usually just take what they need from them without reporting to a supervisor or documenting in the designated spot for item disposal from the cabinet. It would be advisable that every time you take something from the cabinet, you check if anything is missing. If you don't have time at the moment, for example, due to emergency intervention, make sure to return to the cabinet afterward to check if anything else is missing and report to your supervisor or write it in the requisition list for that cabinet. I believe that a list of necessary contents should be pasted inside the cabinet door, making it easy to see what is missing and what needs to be requisitioned.

Depending on the size and type of the facility, the number of required cabinets and their contents may vary to some extent.

It is nice to know how to intervene if someone feels unwell or gets injured, regardless of whether it's a colleague or a guest. It is also dangerous to try to help if you are not trained or at least trained for it. If you are unsure of yourself, immediately contact your supervisor.

It is also important to know the emergency exits in case of a general alarm due to, for example, fire, earthquake, etc. All employees should know the paths to the nearest exits from every part of the building and what to do. It is important not to panic.

When you have no work or very little work, it is difficult because you stand still more than usual, leading to strain on your spine. The easiest posture to adopt is crossing your arms behind your back, on your lower back, as it provides balance to your spine, preventing you from bending forward. This position straightens your spine most naturally with minimal load. It also corrects your shoulders, giving you a balanced and poised stance that exudes professionalism.

Your legs also endure a lot of strain. You spend a lot of time on your feet, covering meters that often turn into kilometers when added up. It's important to think ahead about this. It's best to establish a routine and habit of soaking your feet in warm water for 10-15 minutes after a long day at work and showering while enjoying TV and a snack. Later, when you find some time or before bedtime, elevate your legs slightly higher than your head and body. The sooner you adopt these habits, the easier it will be, and it will impact your comfort and health in the future.

Engaging in activities outside of the hospitality industry is crucial. Everyone needs a psychological "release valve" and should know how to unwind easily. Those working in service, kitchen, housekeeping, and other areas within hospitality face various stressful or mentally demanding situations during their shifts. Some may find their outlet in fitness, swimming, or entirely different hobbies like aquarium keeping or weekend getaways. The key is to find what relaxes, comforts and recharges you for the future.

Vitamins are of great importance. Magnesium can often help with cramps that may occur even at night while you sleep. If you have an issue, for example, with your knee, I recommend wearing a brace. The same goes for the elbow, ankle, and so on.

Proper footwear is essential for the hospitality industry or at least inserts. Comfortable shoes make the job easier. Feet often poses a problem because you spend a lot of time in shoes. Feet get warm, sweat and improper hygiene can cause problems. Consistent and proper hygiene is more than important. It is crucial to thoroughly dry your feet and the areas between your toes after bathing/showering. Neglecting this, even for a short period, can lead to fungal infections. This results in an unpleasant odor, which you can get rid of based on the instructions above. Skin cracking, thickening, blisters, and so-called "corns" can also occur. Use a leading cream, for example. Apply it over the entire foot and always between the toes. Cheap shoes made of fake leather or even plastic are appearing today. This is the biggest problem and source of fungal issues. Fungi can become an unpleasant chronic "illness." The longer you endure it, the bigger problem you create for yourself.

An issue that socks can create is with leg blood circulation because, during long shifts, you should remember to adjust the elastic that visibly digs into your skin in the evening when you arrive. This might seem like a silly detail to mention in a book, but years of work and constant negligence will eventually show on the veins, generally on the feet that may suffer the most in this profession. For this reason, I want to point out every detail I know and have experienced and learned from the older generation.

One of the physical problems is calluses. Unfortunately, they are also a problem that occurs in our profession due to sweat running down the spine. Constant friction while walking and inappropriate underwear leads to a logical problem, inflammation, or irritation ... We will prevent this by wearing, mandatory, an undershirt that absorbs sweat. It also aesthetically prevents sweat from sticking the shirt to the body, which is not appealing to guests. I recommend always having a spare one in the locker, so you can change during long working days, rush, heat, etc.

Nervousness is what needs to be learned to control. For relaxation, colleagues often reach for a glass or two of drinks, which is unacceptable in professionalism. Over time, more and more instances occur of a person lacking self-control. Alcoholism is a topic that is extensive and would take a lot to write about. Hospitality staff is constantly in contact with guests, and "absorbs" a lot, encounters various characters, customs, and cultures, certain issues arise seemingly out of nowhere, and certain problems or gaps lead to moments where many colleagues find solace in a glass. What's worse, even at work! Over time, this can turn into a habit and illness. The natural power of problem amortization is simply lost. This is an issue that needs to be aware of and work on self-discipline and understand what are the core issues and what comes with the job. All the above can be described in one word: tension.

The positive colleagues recognize it and "break" the unnecessary tension by returning positivity to the team and collective. Focus on what you love in this job and enjoy. This is a job that must be loved; otherwise, you are in the wrong place and wasting time. A job that requires great sacrifice but also satisfaction and success for the determined.

Service Quality: Guests expect a high standard of service, including cleanliness, timeliness, and accuracy of orders. Staff should strive to meet these expectations.

Respect: Both staff and guests should treat each other with respect. This includes kindness, patience, and understanding of each other's roles and needs.

Feedback and Improvements: Staff should be open to guest feedback, using it to enhance their service and overall dining experience. Similarly, guests should acknowledge and appreciate the efforts of the staff.

In summary, a positive relationship between staff and guests in the cafeteria is built on good communication, respect, and the common goal of providing and enjoying a pleasant dining experience.

CONCLUSION

Dear colleagues, I hope that in the above lines you have found examples, explanations, images, and perhaps even a reminder that will give you greater courage and confidence in your work. I hope you will eagerly face the challenges of our industry with a smile, and realize that you are artists in your profession; gentlemen with manners, not servants.

Hospitality and service are a fusion of knowledge, experience, psychology, professionalism, and satisfaction, all carried with pride.

Hospitality professionals don't work, they live hospitality.

© 2024, Author Damjan Kralj

[1] Arabica+coffee+plantation&sca_esv

[2] Arabica+coffee+plantation&sca_esv=bb7869262e6227

[3] https://www.google.com/search?sca_esv=bc4b5e46aeab13ae&rl

[4] Robusta+coffee+plantation&sca_esv

[5] Cambodias-ministry-of-agriculture-supports-robusta

[6] https://www.google.com/search?q=robusta+beans&tbm=isch&ved

[7] travel/long-banga-sarawaks-up-and-coming-gem-is-full-of-beans

[8] https://www.google.com/search?q=liberica+beans&tbm=isch&ved

[9] https://www.google.com/search?q=rastavljena+rucka+espresso+aparata&tbm=isch&ved

[10] https://www.google.com/search?q=sito+za+kafe+aparat&tbm

[11] https://www.google.com/search?sca_esv=e9be6bafba5c0576&rlz=1C1CHZN

[12] https://www.google.com/search?q=slepo+sito+za+kafe+aparat&tbm

[13] https://www.google.com/search?sca_esv=94e45fce1d51b060&rlz

[14] https://www.google.com/search?sca_esv=f5ffd29b8bf133f7&rlz=1C1CHZN_en

[15] https://www.google.com/search?q=red+handle+for+decaf+coffee+for+coffee+machine

[16] https://www.google.com/search?q=dust+for+washing+espresso+machine&tbm

[17] https://www.google.com/search?q=dust+for+washing+espresso+machine&tbm

[18] search?q=grejanje+šoljica+na+espresso+aparatu

[19] search?sca_esv=619c697d276fe56b&sxsrf=ACQVn082L

[20] search?sca_esv=619c697d276fe56b&sxsrf=ACQVn082L

[21] https://www.google.com/search?q=cup+of+the+espresso+classic&tbm

[22] https://www.google.com/search?q=americano+coffee&tbm=isch&ved

[23] https://www.google.com/search?q=espresso+machiatto&tbm=isch&ved

[24] https://www.google.com/search?q=espresso+latte+coffee&sca_es

[25] https://www.google.com/search?q=Espresso+ice+latte&tbm=isch&ved

[26] https://www.google.com/search?q=cappuccino&tbm=isch&ved

[27] https://www.google.com/search?q=fredo+coffee&tbm=isch&ved

[28] https://www.googbrle.com/search?q=moccha+coffee&tbm=isch&ved

[29] www.google.com/search?sca_esv=6f22e6a6a58463ac&rlz

[30] search?sca_esv=74899351e738f79e&rlz=1C1CHZN

[31] search?sca_esv=74899351e738f79e&rlz=1C1CHZN

[32] search?sca_esv=74899351e738f79e&rlz=1C1CHZN

[33] search?sca_esv=74899351e738f79e&rlz=1C1CHZN

[34] search?sca_esv=74899351e738f79e&rlz=1C1CHZN

[35] contessa.rs/ugostiteljska-oprema

[36] search?sca_esv=22796dc26b64ca4e&rlz=1C1CHZN

[37] contessa.rs/ugostiteljska-oprema

[38] contessa.rs/ugostiteljska-oprema

[39] search?sca_esv=5debfa16bc1a3c9c&rlz=1C1CHZN

[40] search?sca_esv=5debfa16bc1a3c9c&rlz=1C1CHZN

[41] https://www.google.com/search?q=apparatus+for+making+cold+foam+from+milk&sca

[42] https://www.google.com/search?q=apparatus+for+making+cold+foam+from+milk&sca

[43] https://www.google.com/search?sca_esv=d58752900c71090e&sxsrf

[44] search?sca_esv=09379ecd0b6efd91&sxsrf

[45] search?q=espresso%20machines%20for%20home

[46] https://mccabecoffee.com/products/moka-pot

[47] https://thecoffeestore.co.nz/products/red-handle-tamper

[48] https://www.google.com/search?q=red+handle+for+decaf+coffee+for+coffee+machine

[49] https://www.google.com/search?q=professional+solution+for+cleaning+the+steamer+on+the+espresso+machi

[50] https://www.google.com/search?sca_esv=ba63e9e5b9d099c8&q=thermometer+in+milk

[51] https://www.latteartguide.com/milk-thermometer-coffee

[52] https://www.google.com/search?q=latijera&rlz=1C1CHBF_enME866ME866&oq=Latijera

[53] https://www.google.com/search?q=latijera&rlz=1C1CHBF_enME866ME866&oq=Latijera

[54] https://www.google.com/search?q=diferent+inox+milk+jugs&rlz

[55] https://www.terresdecafe.com/en/cups-and-accessories/1132-joefrex-inox-milk-pitcher-350-ml

[56] https://www.google.com/search?q=kokosovo+mlijeko&rlz

[57] https://www.google.com/search?q=pirin%C4%8Dano+mlijeko&rlz

[58] https://www.google.com/search?q=sojino+mlijeko&rlz

[59] https://www.google.com/search?q=cimet+za%C4%8Din&rlz

[60] https://www.google.com/search?sca_esv=2802dad21c2aa82f&rlz=1C1CHZN

[61] search?sca_esv=b48e549650e04a60&rlz=1C1CHZN

[62] search?q=De+Kyper&sca_esv=b48e549650e04a60&rlz

[63] https://www.kahlua.com/en/products

[64] search?sca_esv=7677bda0a3fd76d6&rlz

[65] https://clickndrink.co.uk/cafe-borghetti-coffee-liqueur-70cl

[66] https://liquorlibrary.co.uk/product/patron-caffe-tequila

[67] Conker Cold Brew Coffee Liqueur

[68] https://www.google.com/search?sca_esv=4fe896d42225783c&rlz=1C1CHZN_en

[69] https://www.google.com/search?sca_esv=4fe896d42225783c&rlz=1C1CHZN_en

[70] https://www.google.com/search?sca_esv=4fe896d42225783c&rlz=1C1CHZN_en

[71] search?sca_esv=1dad59e041ee67d9&rlz=1C1CHZN

[72] search?q=Tequila+Espresso+Martini&sca_esv

[73] https://www.liquor.com/recipes/oaxacan-tail/

[74] search?q=Roman+Holiday+cocktail&sca_esv

[75] search?sca_esv=ad14d01b725f1027&rlz=1C1CHZN

[76] search?sca_esv=ad14d01b725f1027&rlz=1C1CHZN

[77] search?sca_esv=7677bda0a3fd76d6&rlz=1C1CHZN

[78] https://www.google.com/search?sca_esv=4b3fc1098448558d&rlz

[79] https://profesionalnaoprema.co.rs/product/grejac-hrane-beckers-mod-ps-310

[80] https://ugo.rs/oprema-za-brzu-hranu/grejaci-hrane

[81] https://www.expondo.hr/royal-catering-bain-marie-6-posuda-gn-1-3-royal

[82] https://www.google.com/search?sca_esv=4b3fc1098448558d&rlz

[83] https://www.google.com/search?q=display+cases+for+sandwiches&rlz

[84] https://westkitchen.us/collections/refrigerated-display-cases

[85] https://www.google.com/search?sca_esv=4b3fc1098448558d&rlz

[86] https://www.google.com/search?sca_esv=2dffa66a1d9ed396&rlz=1C1CHZN_en

[87] https://www.google.com/search?sca_esv=4b3fc1098448558d&rlz

[88] https://www.allfoodproject.com/en/attrezzatura-per-ristorazione

[89] https://www.google.com/search?q=coffee+art+pictures&rlz=1C1CHZN_en

[90] https://www.google.com/search?q=coffee+art+pictures&rlz

[91] https://www.google.com/search?q=tea+coffee+pictures+free&sca_esv

[92] https://www.google.com/search?sca_esv=dcfda63605418c80&sxsrf

[93] https://www.google.com/search?sca_esv=dcfda63605418c80&sxsrf

[94] https://www.google.com/search?sca_esv=247d501d47960c95&rlz=1C1CHZN

[95] https://www.google.com/search?sca_esv=247d501d47960c95&rlz=1C1CHZN

[96] https://www.google.com/search?sca_esv=247d501d47960c95&rlz=1C1CHZN

[97] https://www.google.com/search?sca_esv=247d501d47960c95&rlz=1C1CHZN

[98] https://www.google.com/search?q=Cardboard%2Fpaper+eco+friendly+straws.&sca

[99] search?q=restoranska+terasa+posle+nevremena&sca

Don't miss out!

Visit the website below and you can sign up to receive emails whenever Damjan Kralj publishes a new book. There's no charge and no obligation.

https://books2read.com/r/B-A-TBEEB-YYAQD

BOOKS 2 READ

Connecting independent readers to independent writers.

Also by Damjan Kralj

1
Guid to coffee culture for Hospitality and Enthusiasts

Standalone
Mastering the Art of Restaurateur: Introducing Skills for Success

About the Author

My background includes hotel and hospitality management, and I have more than 20 years of experience in the hospitality industry/business.

www.ingramcontent.com/pod-product-compliance
Lightning Source LLC
Chambersburg PA
CBHW072225150726
48002CB00005B/1951